383 535

D0453291

Learning Centre

Park Road, Uxbridge Middlesex UB8 1NQ
Renewals: 01895 853326 Enquiries: 01895 853344

Please return this item to the Learning Centre on or before this last date stamped below:

TULLOCH, J. et al
Risk and everyday life

363.37

UXBRIDGE COLLEGE
LEARNING CENTRE

Risk and Everyday Life

John Tulloch and Deborah Lupton

SAGE Publications
London • Thousand Oaks • New Delhi

© John Tulloch and Deborah Lupton 2003

First published 2003

All rights reserved. No part of this publication may be
reproduced, stored in a retrieval system, transmitted or
utilized in any form or by any means, electronic, mechanical,
photocopying, recording or otherwise, without permission
in writing from the Publishers.

SAGE Publications Ltd
6 Bonhill Street
London EC2A 4PU

SAGE Publications Inc
2455 Teller Road
Thousand Oaks, California 91320

SAGE Publications India Pvt Ltd
B-42, Panchsheel Enclave
Post Box 4109
New Delhi 110 017

British Library Cataloguing in Publication data

A catalogue record for this book is
available from the British Library

ISBN 0 7619 4758 2
    0 7619 4759 0

Library of Congress control number available

Typeset by C&M Digital (P) Ltd., Chennai, India
Printed in India at Gopsons Papers Ltd, Noida

Contents

Acknowledgments   vi

1 Introduction: Researching Risk and Everyday Life   1

2 Defining Risk   16

3 Risk and Border Crossings   41

4 Individualization, Risk Modernity and Biography:
   The Case of Work   61

5 Plural Rationalities: From Blitz to Contemporary Crime   81

6 Perceptions of Time and Place in a 'Risk Modern' City   106

   Final Thoughts   132

   References   135

   Index   137

Acknowledgments

Special thanks are due to Dr Helen Lawton Smith who managed the British side of the research project, and in particular organized the programme of high tech interviews via her own list of professional contacts.

The study upon which this book is based was funded by the Australian Research Council.

Parts from the following papers appear in the book in revised or expanded forms:

Tulloch, J. and Lupton, D. (2001) 'Border crossings: narratives of movement, "home" and risk', *Sociological Research Online*, 5(4): www.socresonline.org.uk/5/4/lupton.html

Tulloch, J. and Lupton, D. (2001) 'Risk, the mass media and personal biography: re-visiting Beck's "knowledge, media and information society"', *European Journal of Cultural Studies*, 4(1): 5–28.

Lupton, D. and Tulloch, J. (2002) '"Risk is a part of your life": risk epistemologies among a group of Australians', *Sociology*, 36(2): 317–34.

Lupton, D. and Tulloch, J. (2002) '"Life would be pretty dull without risk": voluntary risk-taking and its pleasures', *Health, Risk and Society*, 4(2): 113–24.

Tulloch, J. and Lupton, D. (2002) 'Consuming risk, consuming science: the case of GM foods', *Journal of Consumer Culture* 2(3): 363–84.

1
Introduction: Researching Risk and Everyday Life

In modern western societies, the concept of risk pervades everyday life. Over the course of the twentieth century and into the early years of the twenty-first, there has been an intensification of discourses emerging from fields of expertise such as science, medicine, law, the social sciences and economics on the nature of risk and its effects upon ordinary people's lives. Various specialized fields such as risk management and risk assessment have developed in an attempt to measure and regulate risk. The news media, for their part, have taken up the warnings of experts about risks and communicated them to their mass publics. They have also reported disputes among these experts that concern risks: how serious they are; who should be blamed for them; what the most appropriate course of action might be.

In this climate of heightened awareness and publicity about risk, how do people respond to, experience and think about risk as part of their everyday lives? In this book we seek to address this question, taking a sociocultural approach to exploring the meanings and significance of risk for 'non-experts' or 'lay people'. This approach acknowledges that understandings about risk, and therefore the ways in which risk is dealt with and experienced in everyday life, are inevitably developed via membership of cultures and subcultures as well as through personal experience. Risk knowledges, therefore, are historical and local. What might be perceived to be 'risky' in one era at a certain locale may no longer be viewed so in a later era, or in a different place. As a result, risk knowledges are constantly contested and are subject to disputes and debates over their nature, their control and whom is to blame for their creation.

The notion of risk and its relationship to and role in contemporary western societies has been the subject of several important writings published in the social sciences in recent years. In sociology the ideas of Ulrich Beck, beginning with the English translation of his book *Risk Society: Towards a New Modernity* in 1992, have proved particularly influential, especially those dealing with the concepts of 'risk society' and 'reflexive modernization' (see also, for example, Beck, 1994, 1995, 2000a, 2000b; Beck and Beck-Gernsheim, 1995). Beck's work has been taken up by researchers across a range of other disciplines including anthropology, criminology, media studies and social geography. The application of the risk society thesis, potentially relevant to any aspect of human experience, to the analysis of a diverse array of social issues in recent times has begun to result in a productive critical reading of Beck's key assertions. Given this influence, we focus in this book on the ideas of Beck in our discussion of how risk is understood and experienced as part of everyday life. The following chapters raise theoretical points put forward by Beck and go on to examine and critique them in the light of our own empirical research, details of which are outlined below. First, however, it is important to provide a brief overview of Beck's concepts related to 'risk society'.

'Risk society'

For Beck, who coined the terms 'risk society' and 'reflexive modernization', modern 'late industrial' societies are in transition, moving from industrial society towards 'risk society' as part of the processes of reflexive modernization. While wealth or 'goods' are produced from modern industrial processes and relating social patterns, so too are 'bads', or risks. These 'bads' include environmental pollution, ionizing radiation and contamination of foodstuffs from such substances as pesticides, as well as social problems such as unemployment and family breakdown. Beck argues that because of the patterns of globalization resulting from late modernization, risks have become more and more difficult to calculate and control, crossing national and socioeconomic boundaries. Risks often affect both the wealthy and poor alike: 'smog is democratic' (Beck, 1992: 36). They also affect those who have produced or profited from them, breaking down the previous social and geographic boundaries evident in modern societies. They are therefore 'glocal': both local and global. Risk society is thus 'world risk society' and risks affect a global citizenship.

Beck's approach to risk varies throughout his writings. At times, particularly in his earlier writings, he presents an empirical realist perspective, in particular when discussing the environmental risks he sees as produced by the processes of modernity: pollution and environmental degradation, for example. Here the term 'risk' is used simply as a synonym for hazard or danger. At other times, he argues the case that risks should be viewed as socially constructed, mediated through the lens of social and cultural processes: that ultimately 'it is cultural perception and definition that constitutes risk' (Beck, 2000a: 213). He has asserted that he takes a pragmatic approach, using realist or constructionist approaches when it suits his argument. Beck elaborates that he views risks as simultaneously factual and moralized/value claims:

> As mathematical calculations (probability computations or accident scenarios) risks are related directly and indirectly to cultural definitions and standards of a tolerable or intolerable life. So in a risk society the question we must ask ourselves is: How do we want to live? (2000a: 215).

According to Beck, unlike in previous eras, risks are no longer easily calculable because of their scale and magnitude. No single institution can prevent large-scale risks or compensate for their effects. Contemporary risks may be minimized, but they cannot be entirely removed. Risks today are also viewed as caused by humans, and thus responsibility and blame is generally levelled for the production of risks. This contrasts with the pre-modern era, in which risks were viewed as the outcome of the workings of fate, or God's hand. Thus, while the processes of modernity sought to bring the world into control, an unintended consequence has been the loss of control via the generation of risks which are both global in their scale and indeterminate in their consequences. Indeed, many attempts to control risks themselves result in broadening the uncertainties and dangers of these risks.

The concept of reflexive modernization, as Beck explains it, involves a questioning of the outcomes of modernity in terms of their production of risks. Beck contends that as a result, public debates constantly feature discussion of risks and their effects, while private lives are dominated by concerns about risks. Awareness of risk, therefore, is heightened at the level of the everyday. According to Beck, the 'risk society' is also potentially a self-critical or self-reflexive society, because anxieties about risks serve to pose questions about current practices. Risk knowledges have increasingly become the domain of 'experts' such as scientists because of their magnitude and, often, their invisibility to the senses. While environmental hazards in earlier days 'assaulted the nose or the eyes and were thus perceptible to the senses' (Beck, 1992: 21) , the 'risks of civilization today escape perception and are localized in the sphere of physical and chemical formulas (e.g. toxins in food-stuffs, or the nuclear threat)' (ibid.). Whereas earlier risks were part of a system of stratification and poverty which was highly visible, today's hazards are invisibly everywhere in the everyday.

In this situation, the power that people's everyday experiential knowledge usually gives them is denied. The hazards are determinable only by others. Lay people are forced to become reliant upon expert knowledges to inform and warn them about risks. At the same time, people have become aware that experts themselves disagree with each other, and they have often made errors in their risk calculations or efforts to control risks. Lay people also see science and industry as producing the very risks about which they are concerned. As a result, the naive certainties of early modernity and its claims to human progress have disintegrated, resulting in individuals' need to seek and invent new certainties for themselves. People are no longer accepting the judgements or advice of experts on face value but rather actively seek to invest their trust in them by assessing their worth and credibility. As a result there are now a far greater number of uncertainties than ever previously existed. Greater knowledge has led in turn to greater uncertainty and a subsequent turn to alternative expertise and knowledge claims.

3

According to Beck, the risks generated by late modernity are also the result of dramatic changes in the structuring of private lives. Traditions that once shaped key aspects of the life course, such as marriage, the nuclear family and lifetime employment, have now been weakened and challenged. In response, Beck argues, there has been 'a social surge of individualization' (1992: 87). People have become compelled to make themselves the centre of the conduct of life, taking on multiple and mutable subjectivities, and crises are seen as individual problems rather than socially based. He calls this 'reflexive biography', or biography that is self rather than socially produced (1992: 135). This does not mean that social inequalities have disappeared. Instead they have become viewed as individualized, perceived as 'psychological dispositions: as personal inadequacies, guilt feelings, anxieties, conflicts, and neuroses' (1992: 100). With the breakdown of traditional certainties structuring the life course, a plurality of new risks are generated – unemployment or under-employment and the destabilizing of intimate and family relationships – accompanied by high levels of anxiety and insecurity.

In the absence of fixed norms and expectations such as those which had structured modern societies (marriage, bearing children, gender roles, employment, social class and so on) individuals are forced to produce their own biographies and invent new certainties, to make their way in life without the guidance of such norms and expectations. This process of individualization is the other, private side of globalization. It involves both freedom to choose, but also crushing responsibility to make the right life choices, a proliferation of new demands upon people facing a growing number and complex range of choices in relation to such issues as education, gender roles, marriage, family formation and employment. These demands themselves create new risks, such as loss of employment, marital and family breakdown, as people seek to juggle the desire for a self-directed and autonomous life with the need for stable relationships and steady employment.

By emphasizing that institutions such as science and industry have come under increasing public scrutiny because of the risks they are seen to generate, Beck demonstrates the ways in which such institutions are blamed for risks. But in his discussion of such phenomena as individualization, he shows how concern about risk has entered everyday life and how individuals are expected to seek knowledge about risks and make decisions based on this knowledge. For him, blame for risk is both projected outwards, as part of reflexive modernization, and taken inwards, as part of individualization. Both processes are different sides of the same coin of reflexivity.

For Beck, the apparent 'irrationality' about risk, which is often identified by experts as a feature of lay perspectives, is a highly rational response to the uncertainties, political processes and disputes surrounding risk. Further, this uncertainty opens up new avenues for political interventions which challenge the institutions and decision-making processes of late modernity, opening them to scrutiny. It is, therefore, also important to recognize that despite the apparently cataclysmic pessimism of Beck's thesis, his is a theory of resistance. Beck ascribes considerable significance to the mass media as a source of information for lay publics, both about risks and about the experts' disputes concerning risks. He himself more than once draws on 'Der Spiegel' as an authoritative source on risk in *Risk Society*. The mass media are an enormously important part of his own thesis of making the invisible visible:

> What eludes sensory perception becomes socially available to 'experience' in media pictures and reports. Pictures of tree-skeletons, worm-infested fish, dead seals (whose living images have been engraved on human hearts) condense and concretize what is otherwise ungraspable in everyday life. (Beck, 1995: 100)

This sense of the *imagistic* power of the media can articulate the intra-professional, discursive divisions within science to allow a 'new democratization of criticism'.

Beck argues that big corporations' use of the media to structure knowledge (power and research) and disseminate it exists in industrial/class-based modernity moves towards risk modernity, even though there are counter usages (by special interest and advocacy groups). It is this overlapping of 'class' and 'risk' modernity that accounts for his occasional comments on the PR-style manipulation of 'gaping' audiences by big business and governments. But also overlapping, in his analysis, are the already existing institutions of the media and the law. He notes the significant effect these can have in challenging the power of the big corporations (in areas like pollution, genetically modified food, smoking, privacy, and so on). In his understanding of the emergence of a new sub-politics, of a new visibility, it is undoubtedly science, for Beck, that most clearly *sees* risks, through what he calls its 'sensory organs': theories, experiments, measuring instruments, which are able to render risks 'visible and interpretable as threats at all' (1992: 162). But if it is science that may provide the eyes, the public will provide the agency for change in a synergy of knowledge and action in the public sphere. No longer, then, will these be 'blind citoyens' but '*active co-producers* in the social process of knowledge definition' (1992: 157, original emphasis). Thus debate is reconstituted in the public sphere in place of modernity's silent collusion of science and capital.

Beck is never simply utopian. He continues to emphasize the continuity of industrial (capitalist) society. He is aware that the very same mass media outlets which he sees as potential stages for the performance of lay/scientific alternatives 'are also and even primarily "servants" of the market, of advertising and of consumption (whether of goods or all sorts of institutionally fabricated information)' and thus they 'possibly produce or exacerbate inarticulateness, isolation, even stupidity' (1992: 193). Yet Beck's is a belief based in a strong sociology of observed intra-professional and intra-political break-up and diversity.

Beck's perspectives on risk adopt a broadly macro-sociological approach that emphasizes the nature of risk at a political and structural level. He has been criticized for his overly rationalistic and individualistic model of the human actor and for his tendency to generalize, failing to pay sufficient attention to the roles played by gender, age, social class, ethnicity, nationality and so on in constructing differing risk knowledges and experiences (see, for example, critiques by Alexander, 1996; Boyne, 1998; Lash, 1993; Lupton, 1999).

In response, Lash (1993, 2000) calls for consideration of the ways in which people respond emotively and aesthetically to risk as members of cultural subgroups rather than as atomized individuals. He points to the role played by unarticulated assumptions, moral values and practices in people's responses to risk. He contends that these are shared and developed through acculturation and are often non-reflexive in that they are taken-for-granted. Lash also asserts that contradiction, ambivalence and complexity are far more a part of the individual's response to risk than is acknowledged by Beck and other risk theorists adopting the risk society approach.

For Lash, aesthetic reflexivity is embodied in such aspects of self-interpretation as taste and style, consumption, leisure and popular culture, and involves the sophisticated processing of signs and symbols rather than simply the accumulation and assessment of 'information'. His approach, thus, argues against the individualization thesis in asserting the importance of group membership and traditional conventions and social categories in structuring responses to risk. He argues for the notion of 'risk cultures' rather than that of 'risk society', which he sees as being too bound to institutions and not acknowledging the role of culture. Risk cultures, for Lash, are less structured and determinate than risk society. They offer fluid and inter-changing ways of viewing risk, drawing on habitual, embodied and affective judgements which are subjective rather than objective.

This more cultural approach to risk is similar in many ways to that offered by the anthropologist Mary Douglas (1992). Her writings on risk, most of which predate those of the 'risk society' theorists, have not been engaged with, to any significant extent, by Beck, Giddens or Lash. Yet they provide an important approach which highlights the symbolic and social aspects of risk. Indeed, central to her theories is the role played by the 'cultural dispositions' which Beck refers to in shaping understandings about risk and identifying risks.

For Douglas, notions of risk are shared within cultures or communities rather than being the products of individual knowledge and perception. She takes a functional structuralist approach in seeing cultural responses to risk as serving to maintain symbolic boundaries within a community, particularly in relation to 'Self' and 'Other', and thus maintaining social cohesion and order. According to Douglas, certain phenomena are singled out for attention as 'risks' in communities due to social and cultural influences. People respond to risk via frameworks of understanding that are acculturated and therefore shared with others within the same cultural context, but not necessarily those outside this context. Risks are related to concerns about legitimating moral principles, and thus the cultural frames used to identify and interpret risks are invariably moral and political. Certain marginalized groups are identified as posing risks to the mainstream community, acting as the repository for fears not simply about risk but about the breakdown of social order and the need to maintain social boundaries and divisions.

Douglas' and Lash's focus on cultural aspects of risk, on the symbolic and affectively-charged meanings which underlie notions of risk, offer an important counterpart to the emphasis in Beck's writings on cognitive judgement, that which is based on the considered and supposedly objective evaluation of 'facts' of risk. They emphasize that risk judgements can never be neutral nor individualistic, but rather are always shaped through shared understandings and anxieties about phenomena which extend beyond the rubric of 'risk', whether this be concerns about controlling and containing the 'Other' (as in Douglas' work) or fear of the 'terrible sublime' of death (as in Lash).

Another difficulty with Beck's contentions is their status as 'grand theories' which have not been tested empirically. As Alexander has contended of Beck's work: 'Broad tendential speculations are advanced about infrastructural and organizational processes that have little grounding in the actual processes of institutional and everyday life' (1996: 134). Lash and Wynne (1992: 7) comment on the multi-layered response to risk on the part of lay people as a form of 'private reflexivity' which, they argue, 'must be the basis for its more public forms'. As this suggests, the development of a questioning of expert knowledges blurs the boundaries between the 'private' and the 'public', for while risks may be debated at the level of expertise and public accountability, they are dealt with by most individuals at the level of the local, the private, the everyday and the intimate. This raises the question, for Lash and Wynne, about where and how the reflexivity that challenges modernity arises, and how it is expressed; that is, 'the sources and social dynamics of forms of reflexivity' (1992: 7). It is here that fine-grained empirical analysis, which is able to explore people's ideas and experiences of risk, may prove useful.

'Private reflexivity': researching lay risk knowledges

Various approaches have been adopted within the social sciences to identify and understand lay risk knowledges. Many of these are quantitative, focusing on measurable attitudes and behaviours that can be statistically analyzed. Psychologists have been particularly interested in assessing and measuring the ways in which people respond to risk. Researchers investigating the psychology of decision-making and judgement use laboratory experiments, gaming situations and survey techniques to understand risk perception, attempting to arrive at a quantitative determination of risk acceptance. Many of these researchers, particularly those drawing on the work of Tversky and Kahneman, have tended to represent lay people as deficient in their abilities, drawing on 'irrational' assumptions when making judgements about such

7

phenomena as risk. In particular, lay people's ability to weigh up probabilities is seen as based on various heuristic processes that are regarded as leading to erroneous conclusions compared to statistical models (Lopes, 1991).

Psychometric research into people's notions of different types of risk have produced a number of conclusions about the ways in which risk responses tend to be organized via heuristics. It has been argued, for example, that people tend to see familiar or voluntary risks as less serious than risks that are new or imposed upon them, and that they are more likely to be concerned about risks that are rare and memorable than those that are seen as common but less disastrous (see, for example, Slovic, 1987; Hansson, 1989; Adams, 1995). More recent research has emphasized the social and cultural differences that are evident in different groups' assessments of risk. Finucane et al (2000) for example, found that among various American groups, whites were less concerned about a range of nominated risks than were non-whites, with white men the least concerned and non-white women the most concerned. They speculate that these differences emerged because of power differentials: those with more power and greater socioeconomic advantage (white men) are less likely to see the world as dangerous than are others.

These findings are valuable in demonstrating that risk perceptions tend to form certain patterns that are shaped by social and cultural norms. As such, they do acknowledge the importance of 'worldviews' and acculturation, rather than reducing risk assessment to individual perception. Such representations of the human actor, however, assume a universal, rational agent who is focused on avoiding risk, or else is ignorant in her or his assessment of risk. Sociocultural meanings tend to be reduced to 'bias', contrasted with the supposedly 'neutral' stance taken by experts in the field of risk assessment, against whose judgements lay opinions are compared and found wanting. Risk avoidance in this literature is typically portrayed as rational behaviour, while risk-taking is represented as irrational or stemming from lack of knowledge or faulty perception.

The growing body of sociological research that has sought to investigate the ways in which people make sense of and respond to specific risks has demonstrated the existence of logics of risk within particular sociocultural and historical settings. Lay knowledges of risk, it has shown, tends to be highly contextual, localized and individualized and reflexively aware of diversity and change. Membership of cultural and social networks and groups is important in the construction and meaning of risk. There is a plethora of research related to HIV/AIDS risk, for example, that has pointed to the highly contextual nature of risk perceptions. People may judge the potential risk of contracting HIV from their sexual partners based on such factors as whether they appear 'clean' or 'dirty'. These judgements are themselves cultural constructions (for example, Maticka-Tyndale, 1992; Skidmore and Hayter, 2000). Central to these assessments are notions about Self and Other. It has been found that people tend to make assessments of potential partners based on such attributes as their social class, appearance, social demeanour and whether or not they are judged to be 'like me'. Decisions about trust are established very quickly on this basis. This research is able to demonstrate that once people have undergone the evaluative process and judged a potential partner as 'safe', their concerns about the risk of HIV infection are dissipated. Sex with that partner is no longer seen as 'risky'. Many other risk assessments are similarly based on concepts of 'Self' and 'Otherness' (Lupton, 1999: chapter 7).

Some of the sociological research seeks to position the lay public as offering an equally valid approach to understanding and dealing with risk as that put forward by 'experts'. It is argued that people construct their risk knowledges based on close observation of everyday phenomena and the behaviour of others around them, including noting the disparity between experts' views. For example Brian Wynne (1989, 1996) studied British agricultural workers' and farmers' responses to experts' assessments of the environmental risks presented by herbicide Agent Orange and radioactive contamination from the nearby nuclear plant Sellafield. In both cases the lay people were concerned about the risks, while the experts sought to reassure them. Wynne's interviews with the workers using Agent Orange demonstrated that their understandings of risk were based on such factors as their experience in using herbicides every day at work and their empirical observations of how the herbicide was prepared and used in the field (counter to official prescriptions of use). In the case of farmers' concerns about radioactive contamination, their views were influenced by the nature of the debate among the experts concerning the level of risk and the experts' demonstrated lack of knowledge about the local issues of farming. While recognizing that they were forced to place their trust in experts (not having the scientific knowledge or training to assess the level of radioactivity), the farmers were also highly sceptical of their claims.

Such risk knowledges on the part of lay publics are viewed as situated rationalities which challenge the views put forward by experts, who themselves may often fail to acknowledge the localized aspects of the generalized assessments of risk that they make. Indeed, Wynne describes experts' assessments as 'optimistic fantasies about behaviour in the real world' (1989: 39). Wynne's and others' research on lay knowledges of risk emphasize the cultural dimension of risk assessments of both the lay public and of experts, including the embedding of knowledges within subcultures and social networks and relationships. It demonstrates the complexities and ambiguities that are part of risk knowledges, and that such knowledges are themselves often open to challenge and revision, based on context.

Other research has pointed to the differences in notions of risk between people living in different social locations or geographical regions. Caplan's (2000) study of British people's responses to the BSE (or 'mad cow' disease) epidemic that affected local livestock, demonstrated how people living in

9

south-east London held views that differed significantly from those living in a large village in Wales. Reactions to BSE among the Londoners were varied, ranging from those who gave up eating British beef to those who took up eating organic beef, to others who decided to take a sceptical approach to media coverage or government advice or to adopt a fatalistic perspective. The people living in the Welsh village were conversant, from personal experience, with beef farming as a way of life. They tended either to discount the risk of eating contaminated beef and thus continued with their usual diet or to seek out knowledge of the beef they were offered in local butcher shops. These people highlighted the importance of 'knowing where the meat had come from' (what area of the country, even which farm) to assist them in deciding whether beef was safe to eat. They tended to place their trust in a local butcher, as someone they felt could supply them with uncontaminated meat. The geographical and social context, therefore, in which people made their decisions about the safety of beef was vital. Londoners had little chance of determining from where the beef they were offered in shops came, and how it had been produced, whereas the Welsh villagers were far more conversant with local suppliers and purveyors of beef, as well as farming methods, and thus were able to invest their trust in those they felt were reliable and 'safe'.

Such research challenges some aspects of the risk society thesis, particularly those contentions that tend to make sweeping generalizations about how 'late moderns' respond to risk. But in its focus on how people respond to specific risks (such as those seen to be posed by science, industry or disease) or their attitudes to expert knowledges of risk, most sociocultural research has done little to enquire into the ways in which people broadly conceptualize and define 'risk' as a concept. Nor has it sought to investigate and understand why people might deliberately take risks rather than avoid them.

The emphasis in contemporary western societies on the avoidance of risk is strongly associated with the ideal of the 'civilized' body, an increasing desire to take control over one's life, to rationalize and regulate the self and the body, to avoid the vicissitudes of fate. To take unnecessary risks is commonly seen as foolhardy, careless, irresponsible, and even 'deviant', evidence of an individual's ignorance or lack of ability to regulate the self (Lupton, 1999). Most of the discourses on risk circulating in contemporary expert and popular cultures portray it as negative, something to be avoided. So too, much of the academic literature on risk represents individuals in late modernity as living in fear, constantly dogged by feelings of anxiety, vulnerability and uncertainty in relation to the risks of which they are constantly made aware. The notion that risk-taking may be intentional and rational seems unacceptable to the psychometric approach. Similarly, in the sociological literature dominated by the writings of Beck, the human actor is portrayed as anxious about and fearful of risk, eager to acquire knowledge in order to best avoid becoming the victim of risk.

Despite the focus on risk in the social sciences in recent years and increasing evidence that high-risk activities such as those involved in 'extreme' sports or leisure activities are becoming more popular (Stranger, 1999), little empirical research has been carried out which has sought to investigate the meanings that people give to voluntary risk-taking. In voluntary risk-taking, the activity in which individuals engage is perceived by them to be in some sense risky, but is undertaken deliberately and from choice. This might be contrasted, for example, with taking part in activities that to the dominant culture are coded as 'risky' but are not perceived as such by those involved. Or by participating in activities which are perceived by participants to be unacceptably risky, but because of their circumstances they have little choice of avoiding, or of which they are unaware at the time of risk-taking.

Studies of American sky-divers (Lyng, 1978), Australian surfers (Stranger, 1999) and, in the UK, young male criminals (Collison, 1996), young men engaging in drinking and fighting (Canaan, 1996) and female boxers (Hargreaves, 1997) have revealed that voluntary risk-taking is often pursued for the sake of facing and conquering fear, displaying courage, seeking excitement and thrills, and achieving self-actualization and a sense of personal agency. It may also serve as a means of conforming to gender attributes that are valued by the participants, or, in contrast, as a means of challenging gender stereotypes that are considered restrictive and limiting of one's agency or potential. As these studies suggest, against the dominant discourses on risk that portray it as negative, there also exist counter discourses, in which risk-taking is represented far more positively. In our own research, we were interested in investigating the positive as well as the negative meanings that may be ascribed to risk and risk-taking.

Our study

What does 'risk' as a concept mean to people and how do they see it as affecting their lives? What risks do people consider most threatening or important to themselves and to members of the society in which they live? Which individuals, social groups or institutions do they see as causing or having responsibility over risk? What evidence is there for 'reflexivity' and a move towards 'individualization' in people's understandings of and responses to risk? Is risk perceived as 'democratizing' in its universal effects, as Beck sees it, or do the old 'modernist' categories of age, gender, social class and so on still play an important role in the ways people understand and deal with risk? What are the narratives, epistemologies, discourses, rhetorical moves, choices of 'rational arguments' and courses of action which people use to organize 'risk' as a cultural concept? What kinds of risks do they chose to take or avoid, and why?

To begin to address these questions, between 1997 and 2000 we carried out an interview study among a group of Britons and Australians. A total of 134 one-to-one interviews (60 in Britain and 74 in Australia) were carried out with a range of people, with an equal number of women and men and a deliberate spread of age groups, educational attainment levels and occupations. Our approach to risk adopted a social constructionist position, which, as we argued above, recognizes that knowledges about risks – both 'lay' and 'expert' – are inevitably mediated through social and cultural frameworks of understanding and are therefore dynamic, contextual and historical. We wanted to explore the global, the local and the privatized aspects of risk as part of everyday life: for example, in what ways people understood the risks, to which they felt they were subjected, to be generated across regional and national borders (a phenomenon of risk of which Beck makes much) or to be local, regional or simply a result of their own personal life circumstances. We were concerned with definitional problems in relation to risk perceptions and information, but at the level of the interviewees' everyday rather than among 'expert' knowledges.

As we noted above, most psychological research, at least in recent times, has recognized the importance of sociocultural frameworks in risk assessment. Our approach differs in both acknowledging the importance of discourse in the construction of risk epistemologies and in emphasizing that *all* risk epistemologies are socially constructed, including those of 'experts'. Rather than drawing a distinction between 'rational' and 'irrational' (or 'accurate' and 'biased') risk assessments, we prefer to concentrate on the meanings that are imputed to risk and how these meanings operate as part of people's notions of subjectivity and their social relations. We also chose to use a qualitative rather than a quantitative methodology in our attempt to identify the role played by risk epistemologies and experiences in people's everyday lives. Identifying the dominant discourses that inhere around risk in the talk of 'experts' and lay people and give it its meaning, is a way of gaining access to the social and cultural frameworks in which we are interested. As our use of the word 'discourse' implies, we are drawing on the poststructuralist understanding of the importance of language in helping to constitute meaning and shape subjectivity.

Our research was designed to be 'glocal', tracing risk perceptions in global/local terms: for example, examining perceived employment, financial and health risks both in global terms (e.g. according to 'economic rationalism', 'globalization', new health pandemics like HIV/AIDS, the internationalization of crime, etc.) and in a variety of regional locations, both in Australia and Britain. The research was concerned with capital's operations in global, local and embodied sites, and with employment biographies that reduce possibilities for a shared burden of risk, but explored this from within the interviewees' everyday contexts.

Of the 74 Australians that were interviewed, 32 were living in the Sydney and Blue Mountains area, 28 in Wollongong and 14 in Bathurst. These locations, all in the state of New South Wales, were chosen to provide diversity. Sydney is the largest city in Australia and the Blue Mountains is an adjoining rural area known for its natural beauty, from which many people commute to Sydney and a place where many 'Sydneysiders' spend tourist weekends. Wollongong is a large post-industrial city near Sydney currently adapting to the gradual erosion of its steel industry, and Bathurst is a small country town about 2.5 hours' drive west of Sydney.

Drawing on Beck's notion of the overlapping nature of 'industrial modernity' and 'risk modernity' (1992: 19–20), the British research focused on three cities which profile themselves as 'post-industrial' (Oxford, Coventry and Cardiff). We tried to select ten interviewees in each city from 'high tech' science-related industries and ten from more 'traditional' occupations (including industrial manufacturing). This was not, we emphasize, an attempt to return to the notion of class and occupation as the principal determinants of sociocultural identity. Rather, these 'work' attributes were examined in the context of other everyday perceptions of risk; and work risks were only elaborated if interviewees chose to do so. However, by choosing an area like Oxford, which is notable both for its leading national high technology profile and for its long-term manufacturing industry (the BMW decision to withdraw from its major Rover cars commitments at the Cowley works was breaking at the time of the Oxford interviews), we could explore a milieu which should have been at the cusp of Beck's 'risk society' overlap.

The same questions were asked of both the British and the Australian interviewees, with two significant additions. Both groups were asked to talk first in general terms about whether they felt life was getting better, first for their compatriots in general, and second for themselves personally. They were then asked to define risk, to describe the ways in which they saw risk as affecting their compatriots and themselves personally: whether they thought such risks had changed in recent times; whether they thought that the risks they took or faced when younger were the same or different now; the sorts of actions they took to avoid risk; the deliberate and voluntary risk-taking in which they might engage; and the ways in which they learnt about risk. Issues of risk in a wide range of areas (environmental, transport, leisure, health, economic and financial, educational, family, work, relationships and so on) were discussed.

The British participants were interviewed after the Australian interviews had been completed. Preliminary analysis of the Australian data allowed us to discern that there was very little concern indeed with Beck's major area of focus: the 'invisible' but potentially 'catastrophic' issues of environmental and biotechnological risk. Yet this area of risk perception lies at the very centre of Beck's notion of a new global sense of risk citizenship and 'risk democracy'. To address this issue of the emerging 'bads' of Beck's risk society thesis in the context of the disappearing 'goods' of his earlier industrial (and welfare) society, we asked the British interviewees direct questions relating to genetically-modified (GM) food (combining issues of environmental and biotechnological risk). Debates over GM food have been particularly vehement in Britain since the late 1990s, receiving wide and frequent mass media coverage (Murcott, 1999). They strike at the heart of dominant ideas about scientific innovation, consumption, health and risk. Another question related to the Paddington (London) train crash of October 1999, in which 31 people died and several hundred were injured. This specific question was asked to get a sense of risk perceptions in relation to spatial mobility (and the new sub-politics recently emerging in relation to the safety and reliability of transport within Britain).

Although the interviews were structured (insofar as the same questions were asked in the same order), considerable freedom was given to the interviewees to shape, emphasize, contextualize and interlink their responses in their own way (for example, by returning in their narrative to elaborate on important issues, find causal links between different kinds of risk, link issues of material consumption and risk, make historical/biographical comparisons of risk and so on). There was, therefore, a strong focus in the questions on eliciting personal experiences as part of an individual biography of risk which was dynamic and reflexive. Given that we had such rich data available to us, we have found that the use of case studies has been a valuable way in which to present our findings, and we chose to adopt this approach in the bulk of our analysis. Such an approach serves well in allowing us to explore the context of people's lives, as well as the history of their experiences, and how these relate to their thoughts and feelings about risk.

The data were analysed for the ways in which the interviewees recounted their understandings, emotions and experiences of risk, with a focus on identifying the dominant discourses structuring their accounts. This approach recognizes that interviewees, consciously or otherwise, choose to present themselves and their thoughts and experiences in certain ways that inevitably access a set of pre-established discourses. Our methodological emphasis, then, is on interviewees' performativity with identities in the interview situation, rather than with 'contradictions' in discourse, as exposed by the expert researcher/analyst. We emphasize here what Bakhtin would call the context-bound utterance of the voice: the notion that through the dialogic narrative of interview situations speakers both establish narrative integration and control, while at the same time incorporating 'past and present experiences and divergent ideologies ... incorporated into a continually developing, ongoing process' (Hassin, 1994: 394). While each individual draws upon their own biographical experiences to impart meaning to events and phenomena, they give sense and coherence to them using these shared discourses that are part of the sociocultural context into which they have been acculturated.

As noted above, most of our interview data are presented in the form of detailed case studies. However, the next chapter departs from this style in providing an overview of the research across the British and Australian interviewees, providing a general rather than specific account of the major themes and discourses emerging in the data. In Chapter 2 we focus on the ways in which our interviewees defined risk as a concept, demonstrating the different meanings they brought to bear in their understandings. We then look at how 'the self at risk' is conceptualized, followed by a comparison of the Australians and Britons in terms of what kinds of risks they saw as threatening their own countries. Analysis follows of the discursive aspects of how risk is understood either as a subject of personal control or out of one's control and the pleasures of voluntary risk-taking. Chapter 3 then begins our case studies approach, by discussing three types of symbolic 'border crossings' related to risk: immigration and diaspora; sexual preference; and aging. The case studies are from the Australian data, illustrating how moving between borders may be fraught with anxiety, fear and difficulties, but in some cases may also be a source of renewal, a chance to remake the self and create opportunities.

The final three chapters provide case studies from the three British cities from which we drew interviewees: Oxford, Coventry and Cardiff. They allow a comparison not only between the risk concerns of Britons versus Australians, but also between people living in different circumstances in the UK: different cities, ethnic groups, social class and age groupings. Chapter 4 presents case studies from the Oxford data, with a particular focus on individualization and work in the age of risk modernity. The case studies in that chapter highlight the plight of insecurity experienced by those working in the precarious 'traditional' industries versus the confidence expressed by those employed in new-style occupations emerging from developments in high technology, which rely on intellectual capital rather than heavy machinery for their power. Chapter 5 focuses on Coventry, this time discussing such aspects of everyday life for the interviewees as their nostalgia for a lost 'community' of wartime Coventry, ideas about capitalism and progress and the 'Others' they identify as posing a threat to themselves, as well as taking up again the idea of 'border crossing' to examine the meanings of risk and risk-taking. The final substantive chapter, Chapter 6, gives case studies from the Cardiff data, looking at the ways in which time and place coordinates influence the risk biographies of 'traditional' and 'high tech' workers there.

2
Defining Risk

As we observed in Chapter 1, one of the main difficulties with current writings on risk in the social sciences based on empirical research is that individual risks tend to be examined. Thus, for example, there are many studies on how people conceptualize the risks associated with HIV/AIDS or with drug consumption or fear of crime. While these studies are valuable for the insights they provide into people's understandings of these specific risks, there are very few published accounts of how people view risk as a general concept and experience, and which risks they see as affecting them over the full range of their quotidian activities. We know very little about how people define risk.

Ulrich Beck has much to say about the role played by risk in everyday life. As we have noted earlier, according to him, awareness and fear of risk is pervasive for the individual in the late modern societies that are in transition to world risk society. His view of this reflexive individual is that of someone who is risk-aversive, sees risks as emanating largely from the institutions of modernity, such as science and industry, is critical of the claims made by such institutions and ready to challenge them, and thus sees risk as a political issue. Indeed, Beck represents the move towards risk societies as generating a new type of politics, generated from the grassroots by lay people who group together to challenge powerful interests and government apathy. Beck's notion of the risk-aversive individual does tend to be an ideal-type. As we have argued, he has little to say about the different ways in which people of different genders, ages, sexual identity or ethnicities might perceive and experience risk. Nor, in much of his work, is he forthcoming on how there might be differences for people living in different countries or geographical locations.

This chapter gives an overview of our data from both the British and Australian interviews and examines the ways in which people conceptualize risk and see it as affecting them as part of their everyday life. In its discussion of broad issues to do with risk, our argument here acts as a basis for later chapters, which go on to examine more specific risks, although constantly relating these to aspects of individuals' everyday lives, attempting to show how they interrelate both with other risks and other knowledges, experiences and concerns. These later chapters use case studies to present our empirical material; however, in this chapter we will take a broad overview. As a result, we inevitably lose much of the richness of detail that case studies are able to afford us. However, we gain a greater capacity to identify patterns of recurring themes and discourses across the entire interviewee group, including not only the identification of similarities but also differences based on gender, age, occupation, nationality and so on. All of the major themes that are identified in this chapter are taken up later in more detail in case studies, allowing us to further illustrate the ways in which aspects of risk understandings and experiences are lived as part of individual biographies as well as via shared beliefs and meanings.

What is 'risk'?

To establish how the interviewees themselves defined 'risk', they were first asked to describe what the term meant to them before further questions elaborated on their understandings and experiences of risk. In responding to this question, individuals proffered a number of different definitions of risk.

For many people, risk involved a weighing up of whether or not to take an action. As a 48-year-old Sydney woman (a management consultant) argued: 'I guess you weigh up the risk of everything you do. There's a conscious or unconscious decision that goes on or some sort of process around a decision regarding what is the risk and how much of a risk you're prepared to take.' Risk as an action or decision with an uncertain outcome was a common definition. Related to this association of risk with uncertainty is the notion of risk as the unknown. Risk for some was defined as involving a loss of security in the face of change, again suggesting an association with uncertainty.

Many definitions of risk described it as a solely negative phenomenon, describing it using words such as 'bad' or 'dangerous', evoking 'fear'. A 44-year-old male health promotion officer from Sydney encapsulated the emotional connotations as well as the need for considered assessment that he associated with the word 'risk': 'Stop, make a judgement, decision-making, fear, nervousness, discomfort, that's what the word risk means to me.' A 35-year-old Wollongong woman (home duties) first defined risk by saying that: 'Risk to me is bad. I feel that you take a risk and I perceive that it could be something that could turn bad.' She later went on to describe risk as: 'Just anything that I could be afraid of'. So too, a 38-year-old postwoman from Cardiff described risks as 'anything that can put you in danger or [be] frightening', while for a 25-year-old unemployed Cardiff woman: '[risk] could be anything – losing your job, losing your home, something awful happening.'

More specifically, risk as a physical danger was emphasized by some people. As a 27-year-old male technician from Wollongong put it: 'Well I might go for a surf and I'm risking my life, you know, looking at rock shelves straight underneath me. I might go motorbike riding, might hit a tree, might get hit by a car crossing the road', while a 31-year-old male engineer, also from Wollongong, argued that: 'To me, a risk is more of a physical or maybe financial thing rather than an emotional thing.'

While these conceptualizations of risk are all very negative, several interviewees noted that risk may have either a positive or negative outcome.

> Well, risk to me is taking a chance at something that will either bring pleasure or gain. It's like a – well, a double-edged sword. It's either going to bring pleasure or gain or it's going to bring you loss or discomfort, and you choose between the pleasure or the discomfort or the loss and the gain. (33-year-old male student, Bathurst)

A 37-year-old Wollongong woman employed as a teacher made distinctions between different types of risks, showing how some risks could be defined as positive and others only as negative. She said: 'Sometimes taking risks is exciting, like, you know, when you're starting a new job it's a bit risky but it's also exciting because it's new, it's an adventure. But if you are driving and it's raining and, you know, the brakes are bad, I don't like risks like that.'

For some interviewees, the danger associated with risk had positive aspects. As a 40-year-old female teacher in the Blue Mountains commented: 'It can mean adventure, challenge, being open to possibilities.' Indeed, taking risks is what defines the human project itself for some. According to a 39-year-old male librarian from Bathurst:

> That's the whole thing about risks – it's apparently what separates us from primates. They don't take risks, but humans do take risks. And that's apparently because of our intellect – we're always testing and all that sort of stuff. You know, to see how far we can go ... I don't think you get an elation [sic] without taking a risk.

Only a small number of definitions represented risk in technical terms as a probability, approximating the 'official' definition which represents risk as a neutral phenomenon which may have a good or negative result. Interestingly enough, these kinds of definitions tended to be proffered by young men working in professional technical occupations, such as in the IT industry, as in the following examples:

> I would define the word risk as meaning the probability of working out all the possibilities of what you are doing, of what might happen and deciding whether when given the probabilities of what might go wrong or right, is it still worth doing. (34-year-old male IT consultant, Oxford)

> Risk means the amount you are willing to gamble in order to – the amount you are willing to lose in order to get a benefit. So, if you want £100 would you gamble £10 or £50, a pound? (31-year-old male IT manager, Coventry)

These dispassionate definitions expunged emotional connotations from the word 'risk' in ways that were not evident in most other accounts.

Risk was also seen as an inevitable part of everyday life for many of the interviewees.

> Life is full of risk and you shouldn't complain about it. There is just a level of risk in walking round. (33-year-old female, company director, Oxford)

Risk is part of your life, that's part of the definition. It's always there – you can't walk anywhere without taking a risk. So it's part of your lifestyle and you have to bear that in mind whatever you do, be it work or otherwise, that you are potentially at risk from a number of things. (41-year-old male, technical officer, Wollongong)

Several interviewees commented that they saw risk as biographical, or different for each individual. They drew attention to the role played by different viewpoints in assessing what is or is not a risk. They recognized, therefore, that risk is the product of a way of seeing rather than an objective fact. As a 46-year-old clergyman from Wollongong asserted:

Risks can be on a very personal level in terms of how you perceive a problem and its difficulties. So risk can be for one person very threatening, and yeah, it can be a risk, where for another human being it's just something they take in the course of life. And so it's a very subjective thing as to what the risks are in doing or undertaking certain actions.

To summarize, we see in the interviewees' definitions of risk, a dominant tendency to categorize risk as negative. The emotions of fear and dread were associated with interpretations of risk as danger and the unknown. Uncertainty, insecurity and loss of control over the future were associated with risk, as was the need to try and contain this loss of control through careful consideration of the results of risk-taking. But there was also evidence in many people's accounts of positive meanings associated with risk: adventure, the emotions of excitement, elation and enjoyment, the opportunity to engage in self-actualization and self-improvement. Beck's and others' assertions that risk is seen by late moderns as a pervasive aspect of life are borne out by the interviewees' views on risk as an inevitable part of everyday life, pervading everything they did. But their portrayal of the fearful, constantly risk-reflexive and risk-avoiding subject is challenged to some extent by the accounts of the positive aspects of risk-taking appearing in the interviews. (We explore this aspect of risk in more detail below.)

The self at risk

Our interviewees were asked to describe the risks to which they felt they were currently exposed, and those to which they were exposed earlier in their lives. In responding to these questions, many people talked about their reckless younger days and how they didn't think about or realize that they were at risk, particularly in relation to such activities as piling into cars and driving around after parties with everyone drunk or otherwise affected by drugs. They commented that looking back from a position of greater maturity and the caution that comes with age and increased responsibility, they now realized the risky nature of their activities. At the time, however, they did not think about or worry about it. This again suggests that many of the interviewees were aware of the subjective nature of risk: that is, that risk knowledges are the products of ways of seeing, rather than being fixed in their meaning.

Many people noted that when they were younger they engaged in more risky physical activities for the excitement of it. As they grew older, the risks they took were of a different nature. This was often even the case for those still in their twenties, as was evident in the account of a 24-year-old male customer services manager from Coventry, who said:

> Oh yes, the risks you put yourself into as you get older are slightly different. Now I wouldn't be stupid with a car, like I was, say, when I was 17. And also going out, I wouldn't put myself into positions where you were going to get into a fight or anything as I would when I was probably 18 or 19. Now, you are older and wiser, I don't know if that is the case but it should be. Obviously the risks do change from where you live and where you put yourself.

The discourse of 'conservatism' was occasionally employed by interviewees when describing their latter-day approach to risk compared with that of their younger days. According to a 38-year-old senior manager from Cardiff, for example:

> Yes, when you are very young, you take a lot of risks, say when you first start to ride a motorbike. When I think of some things I did when I was younger, like that, in everyday life that I wouldn't have considered at the time, because perhaps I couldn't see further to see the consequences. Now I can see and perhaps appreciate the consequences a lot more, I consider them as risks. So I think in many ways I have become more conservative in the last few years, a lot more careful about things.

An important dimension of risk epistemologies that emerged in the interviews was that of a sense of risk as being shared, spread over more than one body/self. This represents a blurring of identity that is little recognized in much risk research in its representation of the atomized risk-avoiding individual. The idea of becoming more risk-aversive was often related to the process of 'settling down' into family life, a life which required one to take more responsibility for one's own safety and to be vigilant in protecting the safety of one's family members. As a 35-year-old male crane-driver from Wollongong commented: 'Looking back now, I used to ride high-powered motorbikes and I did some crazy things on them. And looking back, I know there was a high risk. So yeah, just a lot of sports I've done have been high risk, and I'm lucky to have survived it.' Now that he has a family, this man says he takes more care about physical risks and is more cautious, because his family responsibilities now take precedence. He was very aware of how his own risk-taking might affect his family:

> When I go sailboarding I don't go in as big a surf as I probably would have. I think, you know, I think twice about jumping off a cliff, for example, whereas ten years ago I probably would have just jumped. But that comes with, not so much risk in my own life, but responsibility towards my family. I think of them, then myself.

The notion of a shared risk as part of a close family relationship was put forward by several other interviewees. As a 35-year-old Wollongong woman (home duties) noted: 'The risks that I do take are more of a joint risk, do you know what I mean? Because whatever risks I take my husband takes as well.

Same with him. He takes a risk in getting a new job so that involves me as well, sort of thing.'

This understanding of risk was particularly evident in parents' accounts of their concern about the risks to which their young children were exposed and their need to protect their children. For example, a 34-year-old female council worker in Coventry described how her two children's welfare dominated her thinking constantly.

> You are not just thinking of yourself. You have got to think further, if you have got to go anywhere or do anything, then you have got to think, 'Right, well I have got the kids to sort out, I can't possibly go to college straight after work, because who is going to pick them up from school? How are they going to get home?', and etc, etc. So you have to think around them because it is just not acceptable nowadays for kids to be coming home at six o'clock in the dark from school. And if they have got a club then it takes them later. And I value their lives, if you like, more than my own.

Similarly, a 48-year old female scientist from Oxford, who has two young sons, said: 'I worry about them all the time. The risks I see for them are growing up, drugs, AIDS, jobs, getting university places.' She went on to talk about how she especially feared for them when they were traversing public spaces:

> I don't let them go to town. It is very rare that they are out on their own unsupervised. They do walk in the village to the shop. Harry certainly wouldn't do it on his own but Cameron could do it on his own, now he is eleven. But Harry at seven, he couldn't do it. They are very rarely on their own. Cameron has never ever been in to Oxford without an adult, because I think it has been very risky.

This woman added that her greatest fear in relation to her sons was paedophiles and 'just general psychiatric idiots who just go around killing people and taking people'.

Some men also talked about their fears for their children's safety, as well as that of other members of their family, such as their partner or elderly parents. As a 37-year-old IT supervisor from Coventry recounted, he was particularly worried about the risk of crime:

> Obviously I always worry about crime: obviously for myself and my kids and for my whole family. And I have had a couple of experiences when my mother has been mugged in broad daylight, and that worries me, of course. She is of an age where you can't take too much more of that type of thing, so yes, it is very worrying.

Despite such comments from a minority of men, a gender difference was evident in the ways in which people talked about 'shared risk'. As we saw in some of the above accounts, women with young children tended to describe their anxieties about physical risks to their children. They saw the risks their children faced as important to their own sense of security and wellbeing, and therefore, as also risks to themselves. In contrast, the risks of many men in early- or mid-adulthood and with families to support were financial or related to employment. This is another version of a shared risk, because the future employment of these men affects their family, and they are highly aware of this.

One example is an 38-year-old man in Wollongong, formerly employed as an engineer, who had gone back to university to complete a masters degree in the attempt to find a more lucrative job. He had a family to support and wanted to spend more time with them. He was also keen that his study should pay off in terms of the sacrifices his wife and children had made, such as living in a small, crowded house while he took time off work to study. He noted that: 'The risks I face are in terms of the prospect of not being able to convert all this study into a better job, better employment, or something which doesn't require me to work ten hours a day and never see my family.'

Gender differences were also evident in people's accounts of their voluntary risk-taking experiences. Men tended to describe risk-taking involving sporting activities, travel to other countries or daring deeds. Although women also often mentioned foreign travel as a dominant form of risk-taking in which they had engaged, they tended to talk more about the risks to their children overseas or those they saw as being associated with sexual activity, such as the risk of contracting diseases or becoming pregnant. One example is a 56-year-old female video producer from Sydney, who described how, in the past, 'like a lot of young people, I suppose, I took sexual risks of having, you know, having unprotected sex with people I really didn't know that well. I didn't know their sexual history and took risks of getting pregnant and that sort of thing in silly ways.' Women were also more likely to be concerned about the risks of violence and crime against the person when describing the risks to which they currently felt exposed. As a 39-year-old female artist from Sydney commented: 'I've never felt comfortable as a woman walking around the city at night … I do feel at risk when I walk at night, and I resent that'. (See also our discussion of women feeling at risk from assault below.)

Sexual preference as a source of personal risk, due to violence, discrimination or ostracism, was also raised by a number of interviewees who identified themselves as gay or lesbian. One 44-year-old gay man (a health promoter from Sydney), said that he thought he looked obviously gay, and was concerned about abuse from 'gay bashers':

> People will go out of their way to identify a person who looks like a target and they will purposefully pursue and attack those people. And I know that is occurring in the inner city of Sydney, and when I go and socialize in the inner city, if I'm by myself, I am mindful of that danger … So that's one particular risk that I think I'm confronting: not daily, but regularly.

Gay men were far more likely than others to talk about the risk of engaging in sexual encounters because of possible HIV infection. As the same gay Sydney man recounted, he has been surrounded by the death of lovers and friends from HIV/AIDS:

> I've lost half a dozen of my very close friends to HIV in the last ten years. I've lost two of my partners, one I was living with and one that I'd actually separated from, but nonetheless we had been, we were partners for four years and then he died at a later date. So, I mean, very few people

who are 44 would ever think that by the time they got to 44 that they would have been 'widowed' twice. Because for me the experience of losing both those people was the experience of losing a very dear, very close person in my life. And as well as having lost half a dozen of my very, very close friends through one illness.

Given this man's experience of the tragic effects of HIV/AIDS infection, it is not surprising that he worried about becoming infected himself, even though he was careful to engage in safer sex activities. Similarly, another gay man from Sydney (also 44, and an executive officer), described how he had experienced various 'scares' about the possibility of infection over the past decade. In contrast, of the heterosexuals interviewed, only the youngest tended to mention HIV/AIDS as posing a risk to themselves and they mostly did so only in passing. HIV/AIDS was not conceptualized as a dominant risk for these heterosexuals, but merely one of a constellation of risks.

With the exception of gay men, older people tended to be more concerned about risks to their health than the younger interviewees. However, health risks in the workplace was an issue that emerged as important for some people in industry or trade occupations. These were nearly all men, because few women worked in such environments. One young Oxford man, a 19-year-old apprentice gasfitter, works in an industry in which there is a high level of noise and physical risks from manhandling heavy objects. He stated: 'When I go to work I am conscious that I am going to a high risk environment – you have always got to be on your toes.' A 38-year-old Wollongong man, a technical officer who works in heavy industry, feels that the major health risks to which he is exposed are all in his workplace: 'Asbestos I've been exposed to, um, heights, extreme heights, confined spaces, this type of thing – there's risks in any one of those.' Another Wollongong man, 27 years old and an electrician, said that he frequently takes risks at work to cut corners: 'I take risks all the time. If you can see an easy way of doing it but you know you'll get in trouble you wait until no-one's around and you quickly do it. I risk my life every time I go to work, with electricity.'

Intimate risks, or those associated with love, marriage and the family, were also mentioned by many people (both men and women) as important risks they had faced in the past or recently. People described how entering marriage or a new romantic relationship was a risky undertaking because of the possibility of that relationship failing, and for emotional hurt to ensue. A 48-year-old female consultant from Sydney described the risks she felt exposed to at marriage:

Getting married was a huge risk for me. Well, I was single, I was rampaging around. I lived really quite a good single life. I travelled, I had my own place and I guess it was scary. You know, it was scary to enter into what is meant to be a long-term relationship. And I must say I wasn't a bride that was overly joyful on the day. I found the whole thing overwhelming.

For a 39-year-old male teacher from Sydney, the greatest risk he felt he had taken in his life was his marriage, which at the time of interview had recently broken down:

> I think everybody goes through this – falling in love with someone and taking a risk on not actually putting your all into it and then taking, finding that things aren't working out and taking the risk, in my case of separating, and hoping to work things out and it doesn't happen for one reason or another. And that was the biggest risk in my life, which I don't regret, even though it is very heartbreaking and it's the most physically, like, traumatic for me at the moment. But I don't regret taking that risk. But I suppose that is probably been the biggest risk that I've taken.

Some interviewees also discussed the possibility of hurting friends or family members by doing or saying the wrong thing, or of leaving oneself open to ridicule. A 39-year-old female artist from Sydney talked about: 'the risk of upsetting people. The risk of being rejected by people, disliked, yeah, just sort of rocking the boat. Creating chaos I suppose, making a fool of myself. Feeling exposed afterwards.' A 49-year-old female health educator from Sydney similarly discussed the vulnerability and potential for relationship breakdown that she considered risks in her marital relationship.

> There are some times in personal relationships that I've – I do try and take risks in terms of – like in my marriage relationship. When there's a really touchy issue that I know is going to be, or I sense is going to be difficult to deal with, I feel like I'm taking a risk by actually broaching the subject and bringing it up. So that can be something that I would consider to be deliberately taking a risk. That's an emotional risk really.

Moreover, a number of young women among our British interviewees (mainly of sub-continental ethnicity) saw a major risk finding a partner that their parents did not choose or of whom they did not approve.

For several people, moving to Australia or the UK from another country – or conversely, the chance to move back again against their children's wishes – was the major risk they had taken in their lives. The initial move to a foreign country had involved leaving established social networks, family relationships and all that is familiar, for a strange new environment.

Another specific application of risk to everyday life that appeared in several accounts was the notion of risk as the possibility of failure in financial dealings. Many people discussed the risks that they took in taking on a mortgage to buy a home. According to a 48-year-old Oxford woman who worked as a scientist in a pharmaceutical company, the risks she had recently faced in her life were almost all financial: 'Investments in houses, that is a big one that went wrong. All sorts of other investments are always risks. Pensions are a risk, I don't think pensions are going to be worth what they should be when it is our turn to draw them.' A 28-year-old Wollongong woman employed in home duties similarly noted that: 'When I think about big risks, big risks mean like house loans and stuff like that. I look at risk as more financial – taking risks with money.'

The burden of supporting a young family and its associated worry about risks to employment was replaced for some by concerns in later life about what would happen once they retired. However, some cases emerged of people who became less cautious as they grew older because they felt a lessening of responsibility for their family. This approach was evident in the account of a well-off retired Sydney man in his 60s. He spoke about how he had avoided certain risks when younger and had a young family, but now he did not need to: 'I've reached an age now where I don't have to be cautious any more because my family's all grown up. And I think that you are cautious and conservative when you're younger, when you've got family responsibilities, but I don't think that applies now.'

An older Wollongong woman, now also retired, also spoke of the need to take risks in later life, especially those associated with breaking the mould of the 'nice old granny'.

> The risk that I will speak my truth, that may be a risky business because I may not be seen as that person – that has been, well I wouldn't say sweet, but ordinary, put it that way. I think I'm a little different from the usual grandma. And so there is sometimes a clash of the person, myself being myself with the different roles that I seem to be operating from.

It was clear from the interviews that the risks to which people felt they were exposed were very much phrased through their own position in the life course, their gender, age, sexual identity, occupation and so on. A life-course trajectory of risk-taking and risk-avoidance was described by many people, involving significant risk-taking as a youth and young adult and increasing avoidance of voluntary risk-taking when family and other responsibilities became important. Few people, however, said that they avoided risk-taking altogether, and here again a positive aspect of risk was presented. Some older people noted another change in their approach to risk-taking in their later years, when their responsibilities to others were lessened and they felt less need to be cautious.

The set of questions about personal risks that the interviewees saw as threatening revealed some dominant categories of risk. They included: embodied risks (that is, physical and health risks, the risk of violence); financial risks (associated with employment, supporting a family and retirement); intimate risks (related to romantic, marital and familial relationships); and the risks of foreign travel or migration. 'Shared risk' was again important for people with young children. It is interesting that despite the emphasis of much of the 'risk society' literature on environmental risk, very few people mentioned it when listing the risks to which they felt they had been exposed.

Risks facing Australians and Britons

There is a major difference between the categorization of risks that the interviewees saw as threatening the people living in their countries in general, and those risks they identified as threatening themselves as individuals, either currently or in the past. This was evident from their responses to the question 'What do you think are the major risks currently threatening people living in Australia/Britain?'.

This question evoked responses in the Australian interviewees related to issues of social breakdown, unemployment and national fiscal matters, crime, homelessness, race issues, nationalism and so on. Environmental risks *were* mentioned, although by far fewer people than social divisiveness and structural economic problems. Their responses also revealed the importance of current issues and events in public debate in framing notions of risk. The issue of race was foremost in many of the Australians' minds at the time they were interviewed because of an impending national election and the emergence of a new party, One Nation, led by Pauline Hanson, which adopted racist and discriminatory policies towards Aboriginal people and people from non-British backgrounds. In recent years the issue of reconciliation between Aboriginal and non-Aboriginal Australians has also been very much on the political and media agendas. New acts of parliament have been introduced dealing with native title over land holdings and there has been a call by Aboriginal people for the Australian government to apologize to them for the practice of removing Aboriginal infants and children from their parents, which began in the nineteenth century and continued well into the middle of the twentieth century.

All these issues received extensive media coverage and public debate in Australia in the months preceding the interviews. It is, therefore, perhaps not surprising that divisive racial polices were mentioned by many of the people we interviewed (regardless of their age, gender, area of residence and so on) as a risk to Australians because of its perceived social effects in fomenting racism against Aboriginal people and other ethnic minorities. So too, the politically conservative Australian government's approach to reconciliation between Aboriginal and non-Aboriginal Australians was criticized as posing a threat to the national social fabric and spiritual wellbeing. The views of a 38-year-old female writer from Sydney are illustrative of many interviewees' views of these matters:

> I can see two main areas of concern where Australian society is at risk. I think it is at risk of becoming more insular and less liberal in the inclusive democratic sense of liberal. And that's tied into the whole race divide at the moment, and for me that's tied into the reconciliation process as well. And I think that if that process is not picked up and embraced and really followed fully, I think Australia will miss the boat. I mean there's a real risk of not stepping forward as a brave new nation into the next century. And not healing and not becoming whole, but remaining divisive and petty and out of time, if you like.

The majority of Australian interviewees were also concerned about what they perceived to be unacceptably high rates of unemployment and the resulting effects on social stability and the disadvantaged. Many people also nominated as a major risk facing Australians, the government's approach to welfare and its neo-liberal insistence on self-responsibility for welfare rather than providing for the disadvantaged. As a 33-year-old male student from Bathurst put it, he was concerned about:

the continuing gap, or the growing gap, between rich and poor. The values that are being taught in this country are very hypocritical, mean-spirited, greedy values. And I think those values lead to policies and decisions and actions being taken now that pose the greatest risk to Australian people in the future as our infrastructure and our services and things are sold off, dismantled, taken away, etc. I think that's the biggest risk to Australia.

The notion that society is changing and causing more social problems, was part of a more generalized feeling that Australians were at risk due to changes in moral values and a diminishing of support for the less well off by the government. According to a 46-year-old clergyman from Wollongong:

I think our society at the present time is lacking cohesion, there is a sense in which it's every man for himself. So there is a definite breakdown of corporate compassion, social responsibility, unfair distribution of resources, and fair opportunities in our society. And I personally think that they are the things that are destroying a lot of people's confidence and sense of wellbeing in this country. I think it impinges upon our health right through to our relationships.

As these quotations suggest, it is in people's responses to the question about the risks posed to Australians in general that ideas about blame for risk were particularly evident. The Australian government, above all, was identified as creating or exacerbating such perceived risks as social breakdown, inequity, racism and discrimination. Here the concerns of the interviewees – speaking as a largely privileged group – were often for others rather than themselves: those they saw as being the victims of government policies, such as the unemployed, the poor, immigrants from ethnic minorities and Aboriginal people.

The risks nominated by the British interviewees as facing people in their nation shared many overlaps with those identified by the Australians. Unemployment, a breakdown in notions of community, divisions between groups in society, the emergence of an underclass, drug abuse and crime were commonly identified as risks. However, issues of racism were not as central to most of the Britons as they were to the Australians, even for those who were not white and might be expected to bear the brunt of racism. This difference is most probably because of differences in political climates at the time: race was not on the agenda for public discussion for the British at the time, whereas it was for Australians. (Within a year after the final interviews were completed, the emergence of the 'asylum seeking' issue in both Australia and the UK would have certainly put 'race' back on a common agenda.)

It was noticeable in their discussions about the risks of unemployment that many of the British interviewees emphasized the schism that was currently growing between people with the new marketable skills related to technology and those with more traditional skills in trades. As a 31-year-old female IT consultant from Oxford noted:

I think that the way the world is changing and people maybe not being able to keep up with that is a big risk as well. The way the job market is changing, the way that certain areas in the country

OXFORD COLLEGE
LEARNING CENTRE

27

are very depressed. The way that people have skills in something that maybe is not needed any more and don't feel able to change that if your opportunities-change.

Crime emerged as an issue of concern for many British people, and dominated their discussion to a greater extent than in the Australians' accounts of risk. The Britons commonly engaged in a discourse of nostalgia, discussing how when they were children they felt safe to roam around the neighbourhood, and how this was no longer the case for children, and how once people did not have to take serious measures to protect against being a victim of crime. According to these people, this sense of safety had altered dramatically in recent times. This was evident, for example, in the account of a 34-year-old female council worker from Coventry:

> People never used to lock their doors, from what I hear, they never used to lock their doors. They used to go in and out of [other] people's houses all the while and never worried about being burgled. But now it is a big thing – you lock up and have alarms and have a scary dog sticker in your window to frighten people off, because people are scared of being burgled.

One risk that was discussed by many of the British interviewees but very few of the Australians was that associated with driving cars, reflecting the far more crowded conditions suffered by motorists in the UK compared with the less densely populated Australia. (This risk also was often mentioned by the Britons when they were describing the risks to which they felt personally exposed). The British interviewees, particularly those who frequently commuted by car on major roads, commonly recounted experiences involving perils caused by crowded conditions. A 38-year-old senior manager from Cardiff commented, for example, on the risks he faced in his regular commuting on motorways:

> [On the] part of my journey home, 30 miles along the motorway, I expect to avoid two accidents. Every stretch there is going to be somebody pulling out in front of you or doing something stupid. So I find that the journey home becomes a challenge and avoiding accidents.

Risks related to the UK's relationship to the rest of Europe were also the object of some British interviews. As a 26-year-old male engineer from Coventry noted, job security and employment were his major risk concerns, because he worried about a downturn in the economy. He believed that the government wasn't doing a lot to assist manufacturing:

> [If we are to] be taken into a European single market, it is not an acceptable situation that we should have a lower standard of living than Germany or France, although we have already. With a suitable economic situation we should have the same standard of living as our continental counterparts. So, I think the risks to people in Britain is to be dragged even further behind the rest of Europe and to find that people in Europe have 50 per cent more and have a much better standard of living.

As we noted above, people's assessment of the risks they see as threatening themselves personally is influenced by such factors as age, gender, sexual identity, occupation and whether or not they have children. To these factors we can add aspects that are related to an individual's location in place and space: their nation, town or neighbourhood. In comparing the responses of the Australians with those made by the Britons, the influence of local conditions, including those related to the economy, politics, infrastructure (for example, the road system) as well as geographical location (the UK's relationship to the rest of Europe) are clearly integral.

The notions of control/non-control

For most of our interviewees, British or Australian, the idea of risk encapsulated the notion that, to some extent at least, risks could be personally controlled. A male 46-year-old teacher from Wollongong, for example, argued that one could control all risks, as long as the appropriate information was sought and actions taken.

> I think you can control all risk, personally I think you can. But you've got to take certain steps towards it. For example, I think you've got to be prepared. You've got to be aware of everything. You've got to have good information: if you've got bad information you're going to come to grief. If you've got good information and you're aware of the things and you make good logical decisions, risk is quite calculable and it's also quite manageable.

Associated with this idea was the belief that people should take responsibility for risk, and act to avoid it rather than blame others or expect others to protect them. This approach to risk and responsibility was particularly the case for people with significant cultural and economic capital, such as members of the well-educated middle-class. According to a 31-year-old Coventry man (IT manager), for example:

> I think people are altogether worried about the fact that they consider themselves to be put at risk by other people when in fact you put yourself at risk, nobody else does it for you most of the time. You get in a car and you are risking somebody driving into to you. If you stick your finger in a socket you are risking being electrocuted ... I think people have become or are becoming too reliant, too willing to put the blame on somebody else rather than themselves where risk is concerned. I think you should accept a certain level of risk and when you do anything you should accept it.

The idea that risks are 'there' and it is a personal choice whether one decides to take that risk was put forward by several people.

> Like the risk has been put there, it's up to us whether we take it. Like it might be like violence is caused by the people that are doing it, but it's our risk whether we want to get involved in it. We're risking like, whether we want to walk out in the street or leave our house unattended at night. You know, like there's more risk now than there used to be. Like you could walk out with your door open before type thing. But it is our choice to leave, to take the risk to leave our house unlocked or you know, whatever. (28-year-old woman, home duties, Wollongong)

However, there was a difference in most people's accounts in conceptualizing control when applying it to risks facing oneself as an individual and risks facing one's nation. Those risks regarded as personal were viewed as more able to be controlled, because they were regarded as a product of choices made by an individual. To smoke or not to smoke, to take out a mortgage or continue to rent, to marry or stay single; these were the types of choices that people saw as within their personal sphere of influence. According to most people's thinking, the risks associated with such choices could be managed to a great extent. As a 31-year-old female IT consultant from Oxford commented:

> I think with health risks you have a degree of control over them, because you can alter your lifestyle or you can test yourself to know whether with your cholesterol – like cholesterol, there is a high risk of cancer if you have got it in your family or whatever. You can have a degree of control and there is also a degree of it outside of your control. Things like being attacked, then yes, you have a degree of control there as well because you can choose the area which you live. You can choose whether or not you walk around at night. You can choose the areas you drive in, but again there is always going to be the freak thing. I don't think you can stop it happening, but I think you can change your chances of it happening.

This woman then went on to detail how she attempted to control the risks to which she felt she was exposed:

> When I go up to London to see a friend then I am quite careful about the areas that I am walking around in. You know, I will stop and think about it. And I will think quite carefully about what I eat and drink, and try and stay healthy and try and to do some exercise, all those sorts of things. I will see where possible I can minimize risks, whether or not I will still do what I want to do. So I would *not* drive on the motorway because I would have a risk of being in a car crash, or I would *not* go on a train because loads of people have died on the trains recently.

People were highly aware, however, of the risks imposed upon them over which they had little control, and which therefore could not be managed effectively, but rather had to be left to fate to some extent. As a 34-year-old male IT consultant, living in Oxford said, he felt at risk flying in aeroplanes because 'it takes things out of my control [because] I am not really flying the plane'. Another example is the comments made by a 31-year-old engineer from Wollongong, who said of the risks he faced at work that:

> The risks in industry are that you're always worried about something happening that you've got absolutely no control of, that you're not even aware of, and you're just one person in the wrong spot at the wrong time so to speak ... To me that's probably the worst sort of risk because that's just out of your control. No matter what you do you're putting essentially your health or wellbeing in someone else's hands. You've sort of got to rely on other people's skill or work practices or whatever – even their own perception of what they think a risk is or what's not a risk. That's sort of why I prefer risks where I've got some control.

The well-educated and well-off have less to fear from such broad social problems as unemployment than do those of less cultural and economic capital. A common consensus among this group was that, in the current unstable and globalized labour market, anyone's job could be at risk. Secure lifetime employment was no longer a certainty, even among highly-educated professionals. However, it was noted that people such as themselves were more easily mobile than the less advantaged, able to find new jobs if they lost their old ones. As a 25-year-old man from Coventry, who is a patent attorney, noted:

> I suppose it has moved from the stage where you did have a job for life in certain areas, to a stage now where if you have got the requisite skills in the right kind of industry, you won't have

the same job for life but you might have *a* job. If you are unfortunate to be in an area that is in decline, such as ship building, then you might have problems, you'd definitely have problems. I suppose if you move into an age where it's knowledge rather than strength is what counts in getting a job, those people who don't have the qualifications are going to the ones who have the problems.

Many people such as those working in burgeoning professions such as in the IT industry or marketing appeared willing to take risks in relation to their employment and livelihood: leaving a good, well-paid job to start their own company, for example. They could do so, they noted, because they had the safety-net of their own, highly-marketable skills and knowledge to protect them from unemployment and penury. One 25-year-old marketing manager had started her own marketing business at 21 years of age. She noted that this was 'a big risk – probably the biggest risk I have ever taken'. At a similar time she had invested in the property market by buying herself a flat, and again considered that a major risk because of possible fluctuations in the market. Her playing with the 'market' continued; at the time of interview she was planning to give her notice with one of the strongest marketing companies in Britain. Although she characterized this move as 'quite a big risk', she later described it as 'almost a little bit of a safe risk, if there is such a thing' because of her confidence that she would do well in her new post:

> I could stay here but in two years time when I wanted to move, I may not be able to find another job. It was a big decision to make, but that is probably the biggest risk ... I go for that sort of risk because that is to better myself as in individual, my social life, my career, so that is a risk I am prepared to take because in the long term the future prospects are much better, so I am happy to do that.

Here again, issues of gender and age affected people's responses. Men, particularly those who were younger, generally expressed more confidence in being able to control their lives than did others. This was particularly evident in their discussions of how much at risk they felt of being a victim of crime upon the person. As noted above, women expressed greater fears about personal safety, while several men described themselves as physically robust, or 'beefy' in the words of one Coventry man, and thus less susceptible to assault. In contrast, many women portrayed themselves as vulnerable and prey to attack. They commonly mentioned 'walking down country lanes', 'deserted roads' or 'in the city centre' at night as experiences where they felt strongly at risk from attack. One example is a 17-year-old Coventry woman (a finance assistant), who described her strong fears of travelling alone at night:

> Sometimes I feel very insecure when I am alone in the town, even if it is just on a Saturday afternoon. Sometimes, I get a really bad feeling that something is going to happen but then it doesn't. It is like when I have been down to the pub or something, I have dropped my friend off at home and then I have got to drive home on my own and there is no-one on the road and my mind starts to turn and starts to work and I imagine what would happen if. Then it becomes a risk where perhaps before it wasn't a risk, I feel as though I am taking a chance going home on my own because something might happen.

People's cultural capital in terms of their educational background and marketable skills also influenced their responses about the risks associated with employment. In sharp contrast to the confident risk-taking professionals was the 36-year-old single mother working for the council as a tenants support officer in Coventry. Losing her job would be a disaster for her family, she said:

> Jobs are not always secure. Years ago you used to come and work for the council and it was a job for life but that has vastly changed now. I am a single parent looking after my two kids with some sort of financial support from my dad and if I was to lose my job then my house would be at risk and my mortgage, where we live, our livelihood really. So that it is important to me to maintain a job and give them a standard of living.

Sometimes events in people's lives were such that they had come to realise the extent to which control over risk was illusory. This was the case for a 54-year-old Bathurst student. She was suffering from a degenerative illness and worried about how her illness will affect her as it worsens. She discovered recently that one of her sons was taking speed, and was traumatized about the fact that her husband had threatened to leave her for a younger woman. She saw none of these risks as controllable on her part:

> I want to be able to become fit again. I feel that if I could have some form of control over my fitness, or some sort of regime that I knew how to control it and cope with it, not overdo it because I tend to overdo it all the time. I think I could probably cope, but that I don't have control over – I don't have control over my husband and I don't have any control over my sons. So no, I don't really feel that I have control over the risks that are confronting me.

Indeed, several people expressed a fatalistic approach, arguing that one has to accept what life throws at one, and that many risks are simply beyond the individual's control.

> I think you can assume some responsibility for risk, but also I think I'm fairly fatalistic about it. Some stuff will just happen no matter what choices you make. Yeah, so in a way the choice only gives you the illusion of control. I mean, stuff will happen regardless. (38-year-old female writer, Sydney)

> Well, people make their own choices generally about what they want to do with their lives and their bodies and their relationships. But sometimes the unexpected can happen – there's always an element of chance. There are risks that can happen that you didn't even know existed until they actually happen. (45-year-old unemployed woman, Bathurst)

We see a tension in these accounts between the notions of control and non-control over risks. Risks which are defined as subject to personal responsibility are those which are largely seen to be controllable. Risks which are conceptualized as external to personal decisions or actions tend to be viewed as non-controllable, as more susceptible to the vagaries of fate. Late modern notions of risk, to do with responsibility, blame and control are here interlaced with pre-modern ideas about fate and lack of control.

The pleasures of voluntary risk-taking

As we suggested above, although risk was frequently conceptualized as a highly negative phenomenon, many people evinced the view that there were positive aspects to risk-taking. This was particularly the case when people felt that they had some choice over taking risks: that they were voluntary. The ways in which people conceptualize and describe the pleasures of voluntary risk-taking are worth further analysis.

When analysing the interview data, it became clear that metaphors of spatiality were an important conceptual tool employed by people when they talked about the voluntary risk-taking in which they engaged. When asked about the kinds of risks they took and why they did so, the research interviewees commonly expressed the notion of risk as located outside a defined boundary. For example, a 35-year-old woman who lives in Wollongong and works in the home, said that: 'I think risk is stepping out of your comfort zone and leaving familiar territory and going off into the unknown, or doing something you haven't done before.' A 46-year-old clergyman, also living in Wollongong, expressed his idea of risk-taking as transgressing the barriers defining safety and security. In his case, as a minister of religion, risk-taking involves taking a public principled stand on social matters that he thinks need redressing. Again, he used spatial metaphors to express this, drawing in particular on those connoting a war zone. He said:

Well, personally, I think that life would be pretty dull without risk. I'm a risk junkie in some respects, in as much that I like wandering out there in no man's land, behind the barriers. Every now and again it's worthwhile to retreat back in behind the safe barriers. But life would be pretty dull without risk, and I enjoy those opportunities.

As these accounts suggest, risk lies outside the 'comfort zone' and familiar territory. It represents that which lies beyond the known: 'no man's land'. Lyng's (1978) writings on 'edgework' also employ a vivid spatial metaphor to describe risk-taking. To engage in the edgework associated with risk-taking, the term suggests, is to teeter on the brink of something, to balance precariously on a sharply defined boundary, to peer into the abyss. Indeed Lyng emphasizes that edgework takes place around cultural boundaries such as those between life and death, consciousness and unconsciousness, ordinary and extraordinary.

In some of the interviews, the notion of risk-taking as imparting a momentum to the trajectory of one's life, facilitating movement from an ontological stasis, was evident. This appeared in the words of a 54-year-old woman in Bathurst, a university student, who noted that: 'I'm not saying there are things out there that we shouldn't do, but if you don't take a risk in your life somewhere along the way, I don't think you'll get anywhere. I think you'll just stay put.' This idea of risk-taking as movement extends the spatial metaphor temporally. One crosses boundaries when taking risks, moving from one space to another. It is risk-taking that impels movement and progression. In this woman's interview, she described risk-taking as a form of feminist protest against the conventions that restrict girls and women in their lives. In her case, growing up in the country in the 1950s, such restrictions were imposed particularly by her parents: 'Being a girl, you have to take risks by trying to overcome the taboos that [limit] women.' In her own life, she said, as a young girl she chose to deliberately court risks when riding her horse, and also by taking up cigarette smoking and drinking alcohol. In so doing she was 'going against [her] parents' wishes' and thereby challenging restrictions they sought to impose upon her.

A 60-year-old unemployed man also living in Bathurst discussed how, in his younger days, he enjoyed riding in rodeos, a physical activity that posed great threats to life and limb. He described the benefits and pleasures he saw as gaining from this experience:

> I'm thinking probably the most focused risk-taking, where you really can't predict what might be the outcome of the activity at all, is riding in a rodeo, which I did over about a two-year period, and each experience is unique and absolutely unpredictable. What it is that you get from success is a degree of personal satisfaction and self-esteem as a result of taking, accepting a risk and being successful. And if you said to me, you know, 'Is it worth it?', I'd have to say 'Yes!'. It's part of the whole process of becoming the person that you finally finish being, presenting oneself in another way.

This man's account is clear about the ways in which he conceptualizes this particular risk-taking activity as contributing to his sense of accomplishment, and indeed, to the continuing process of developing self-identity. For him, rodeo-riding was a means of testing himself and demonstrating to himself the limits of his skills. So too, Lyng (1978) found that for the edgeworkers he spoke to, who engaged in parachute jumping, the notions of 'self-realization', 'self-actualization' and 'self-determination' were commonly claimed as goals of their dangerous physical activity.

The discourse of self-improvement in relation to risk-taking bespeaks the cultural importance placed on knowing and monitoring the state of one's self, on movement and progression of this self, on flexibility and adaptability. As a 39-year-old Sydney man (working in the theatre), put it: 'I don't think that you can live life fully without placing yourself in a risky situation. I don't think that you can really fully find your own full potential without taking risks.' The boundaries here concern the boundaries of the self: that which is deemed possible in terms of self-realization and expanding one's life experiences.

Risk-taking is also fundamentally associated with emotion. To be confronted with risks that one does not choose to take is to experience 'fear, nervousness, discomfort', as one of our interviewees quoted above put it. But to deliberately take a risk may be also to seek a heightened degree of emotional intensity that is pleasurable in its ability to take us out of the here-and-now, the mundane, everyday nature of life. A 39-year-old male librarian in Bathurst talked about the pleasure he experiences when surfing in rough seas in these terms:

> Sometimes you want to take a risk because of the adrenalin buzz and all that sort of stuff. Sometimes it's unintentional, but still, when you're in the throes of it, like being dumped by a

huge wave, you still could be potentially killed or whatever, but it's still a great rush … Even though you might be dumped by a wave and you might go 'Wow, yeah, I can feel the forces of this wave just ripping through me!'. And it's ecstasy sort of stuff, it's still a discovery. And that's where you get the elation, and I don't think you'd get elation without taking a risk.

This man's words, which impart an almost erotic meaning to the experience of surfing, suggest that an important aspect of risk-taking is the opportunity it offers to allow a 'swept-away' feeling. Risk-taking is a form of release in his account. His representation of the joys of risk-taking in surfing are echoed in the words of surfers interviewed by Stranger (1999), who also referred to the sensuality of the ultimate surfing experience, the link they perceived between thrill, desire and danger. Those surfers commonly referred to the sublime nature of feeling 'one with the wave' through their exploits.

These accounts suggest that participating in activities that are coded as dangerous or 'risky' can bring an adrenalin rush that allows aficionados to escape the bounds of the rational mind and controlled body, to allow the body's sensations and emotions to overcome them for a time. There is a sense of heightened living, of being closer to nature than culture, of breaking the 'rules' that we see society as imposing upon us. Here again selfhood is important. The emotions produced by risk-taking are seen to give access to authenticity of selfhood by confronting the barriers of convention or social expectation.

We discussed above the binary between control and non-control that emerged in interviewees' accounts of risk. This binary emerged again in some of the accounts privileging the emotional intensity of risk-taking, where there was a sense that the pleasures of risk stem from loss of control over the body. It is clear, however, that there are few situations in which people totally lose the desire to retain some degree of control over their bodies. This is evident in the account of a 51-year-old businessman living in Sydney, who enjoys sailing on the city's harbour in his spare time. He said that he saw the risks he took as part of this pursuit to be within his control and therefore as pleasurable. He drew a clear distinction between voluntary and involuntary risk in his account:

I think that [sailing is] associated with a sense of control and it's a calculated risk, you see? I mean, in some sense it's very controlled because you have control over your welfare, as opposed to sitting in an aeroplane with someone. I think maybe that might be as good an example as anything of my understanding of risk, where your wellbeing is in the hands of someone you don't know. And yet I suppose the general population would accept driving a bus or a ferry or a plane or public transport or a taxi driver, and accept it and feel quite safe. I guess that's where I feel at risk, when I'm not in control.

This man later in the interview went on to describe how he feels in control when facing risks in sailing:

On the one hand you don't have control of the elements, but then you do have control over the preparation of your vessel and you do take it on as an intellectual challenge, to deal with the problems that are going to arise. And I suppose only a challenge because there's a risk involved. So there you have it. I mean, you know, I suppose here I think back to situations where you end up in an extreme situation. Where you've gone out for a nice sail or to get from A to B or whatever, and it starts off fine and then suddenly a storm comes along and suddenly it's not so pleasant any more. And then it gets downright unpleasant and then you're going to get cold and then you're going to start worrying about the boat and things go wrong. And so then, you know, it gets a risky sort of situation. Now the thrill comes from having to turn around a position of being, feeling vulnerable, uncomfortable, unhappy and deal with it and take control.

A 39-year-old male theatre worker in Sydney also talked about the pleasure of control over danger as part of risk-taking in a similar fashion. Although he represented himself as a cautious type, taking care to drive carefully and look after his health, he said that there were certain times when he allowed his caution to slip somewhat. This man works in production, and must climb ladders on occasion to check lighting arrangements. He said that he had a fear of falling off ladders and was generally very careful when using them. But sometimes he found himself testing his fear and deliberately taking risks: 'Occasionally when I'm up on a ladder I get a bit reckless and I find myself balancing up in the ceilings of theatres on lighting bars, having stepped off the ladder onto the lighting bars. And I'm actually quite scared about what might happen and what the result might be.' He went on to explain what he got out of this risk-taking: 'Balancing on a bar thirty feet off the ground and continuing to work for a little while, and then escaping from that situation and making your way back down to some sort of solid floor, can give me a feeling that I'm very much in control of my body. And that is a very nice feeling really, I like that feeling.'

Voluntary risk-taking, for these people, is inherently implicated in their notions of the boundaries of their bodies, how far they feel they can push themselves, how well they can conquer their emotions of fear and feelings of vulnerability. They are engaging in edgework that allows them to experience an intensified body awareness but that also contributes to their sense of being able to control their bodies. Even within the meanings of edgework, control of the body remains a central preoccupation. Edgework is also characterized by an emphasis on skilled performance of the dangerous activity, involving the ability to maintain control over a situation that verges on complete chaos, that requires, above all, 'mental toughness', the ability not to give in to fear (Lyng, 1978). Cultivated risk-taking in this context is seen to provide an opportunity for individuals to display courage, to master fear, to prove something to themselves which allows them to live life with a sense of personal agency.

Concluding comments

It was evident from the interviews that different ways of asking about risk understandings and approaching risk perceptions from different angles, produce different discourses on risk. When asked to define the concept of 'risk', the major discourses used by our interviewees centred around the notion of risk as negative, frightening, involving taking a step into the unknown but also a degree of rational judgement and choice on the part of the individual concerning whether or not to take this step. Once this choice has been made, however, there is a sense of fatalism about what may then happen, a loss of control over the outcomes. Risk was predominantly represented as an ever-pervasive part of life and also as strongly tied to individuals' life situations, which were seen to both expose them to certain risks and to influence the ways in which they viewed phenomena as being risks or not.

Beck (2000a: 215) argues that what he sees as the 'logic of control' which dominated early modernity, a desire to exert control over the conditions of life, and a belief that this can be done using rational processes, has become eroded under the conditions of late modernity. Control has become an illusory hope because of the very nature of contemporary risks: their seriousness, their incalculability and unpredictability. But it would appear from our interviewees' accounts that early modernist beliefs about control over risk still dominate people's ideas, as do some pre-modern notions. Many risks are categorized as non-controllable by the individual, but this is because of fate, or the actions of others which are themselves beyond the individual's control, rather than because the risks are seen to be incalculable or global.

The risk actor emerging from these discourses in many ways approximates the fearful and rationally reflexive subject of Beck's writings, who is both highly aware of the pervasiveness of risks and seeks control over them. It was clear from several accounts, however, that risk was also seen in some ways as positive, in terms of voluntary risk-taking for purposes of personal gain, be that financial or as a contribution to a more exciting life or self-actualization, or simply as part of the human project. Here another version of the reflexive actor in response to risk emerges, an actor who may well be somewhat frightened of the outcome of risk-taking but is also willing to take some risks because of possible benefits.

Our study revealed three major discourses employed by our interviewees to describe the pleasures and benefits of voluntary risk-taking. The discourse of self-improvement was employed to describe the importance of working on the continuing project of the self through taking risks, while the discourse of emotional engagement drew on a neo-Romantic ideal of the body/self allowed to extend itself beyond the strictures of culture and society (Lupton, 1998). The third discourse, that of control, in some way counters that of emotional engagement in privileging control over one's emotions and bodily responses as a valued aspect of engaging in risky activities. All three discourses represent a life without risk as too tightly bounded and restricted, as not offering enough challenges.

These discourses are also underpinned by contemporary ideas about the importance of identity and selfhood. The notion of risk-taking as contributing to self-development, self-actualization, self-authenticity and self-control, is part of a wider discourse that privileges the self as a continuing project that requires constant work and attention. Risk-taking, in this context, becomes a particular 'practice of the self' (Foucault, 1988), a means by which subjectivity is expressed and developed according to prevailing moral and ethical values.

Further, the use of spatial metaphors in talk about risk-taking demonstrates the importance of the concept of cultural boundaries in thinking about the body, self and social relations. Douglas' (1966) work on purity and danger highlights the integral role played by conceptual boundaries in constructing ideas of Self against those of the Other. She argues that it is particularly at the margins of the body and society that concerns and anxieties about purity and danger are directed. Because margins mark and straddle boundaries, they are liminal and therefore dangerous, requiring high levels of policing and control. This is why we tend to think of risk-taking as involving the transgression of boundaries; and why there may be an additional sense of self-improvement when policed boundaries are crossed. That which lies beyond the boundaries of the self – that is, the domain of Otherness – is risky. Risk is dangerous, but also exciting, in its lack of certainty and challenging of the borders between the known and the unknown.

When describing the risks to which they felt personally exposed, the interviewees emphasized the perceptual nature of risks, particularly in relation to their own life course. A reflexive awareness was evident in their comments concerning how risk is understood and perceived in different ways for different people or social groups. They saw risk perceptions as dynamic, changing for themselves over the course of their lifetimes or even from day-to-day as priorities changed. They sketched out a trajectory in which they presented themselves as exposing themselves to greater risk when in their adolescent years or early adulthood, and, along with 'settling down', becoming more aware of and cautious about risks, but then, with greater age, perhaps taking more risks once again, having found themselves freed of some limits to their risk-taking.

In many of the interviewees' responses about personal risks, there was little sense of external forces producing risks. The scapegoats for risks identified by Beck – big industry, science, the government – do not appear in most of these. Rather, the interviewees tended to represent themselves as autonomous actors, rationally making decisions about which risks they choose to take or recklessly taking risks without at the time 'realizing' that they were, indeed, risks. They do appear to have taken on the tenets of individualization as they are described by Beck in representing crises, fears and anxieties as self-produced and individual problems, the products of 'personal biography'.

However, when discussing those risks to which they feel that people living in their countries in general are exposed, the interviewees shifted their focus. They no longer tended to individualize risk, seeing it as isolated from social inequity. On the contrary, an overwhelming trend in their responses was to politicize risk, emphasizing the production of social inequity via deliberate government strategy or neglect. Contrary to Beck's assumptions, individualization co-existed with an older modernist discourse that recalled Marxist critiques of the state. The interviewees' trenchant criticism of government and its production of risks to the social fabric – in allowing welfare systems to break down, unemployment to worsen, racism to continue and crime to flourish – suggests not only a reflexive approach to risk but also the hermeneutic approach for which Lash argues. The interviewees were reflexive in offering a critique of government and its policies, positioning it as the structural cause of risks facing their countries. Many were hermeneutic in expressing their disquiet about a society dominated by neo-liberal tenets in which inequality is not dealt with as once it was and about the direction they felt their country was taking as a result of government policies and responses to social problems.

Notions of nationhood underlay the interviewees' affective response to such risks. The Australians' responses, for example, suggest disillusionment and disappointment that the ideal of fairness for all, which is a vital part of the imagined Australian national ethos, seems to have given way to social divisiveness and a lack of concern for the underprivileged. The British worried about their place in Europe compared with other EU countries and maintaining a standard of living and education that were seen to be appropriate for their nation. There was also a prevailing sense of a 'widening of the gap' between (knowledge) risk and the new poor, which was differently inflected according to age and acquisition of the 'new economy' skills, but which in nearly all cases – on either side of the 'new divide' – led to an increasing fear of crime.

Importantly, people's concerns about risk were far from the acid rain, Chernobyl effects and 'mad cow' disease which have preoccupied the Europeans on whose behalf writers like Beck speak. Only a minority of our interviewees (slightly more in Britain than Australia) identified environmental problems as major risks, either to themselves personally or to people in their countries in general. For the Australians there was little talk about the effects of 'globalization' in creating risks for Australians: rather, the causes of risk tended to be located within Australia. Some of the British, in comparing their country with other EU nations, did evince a greater awareness of the risks involved with globalization and membership of economic entities beyond the geographical borders of their country. This suggests that the 'risk society' thesis is ethnocentric in its sweeping claims, failing to recognize the diversity of national and sub-national interests and concerns. In later writings, Beck (2000a) has come to realize this shortcoming, and has called for research which, for example, explores cultural differences in risk definitions and perceptions between countries in Europe.

We noted above the importance of concepts of boundaries and borders that give meaning to risk and to voluntary risk-taking. The next chapter goes on to focus specifically upon an aspect of risk experience that involves the crossing of boundaries and borders, both literal and symbolic. In some cases, this border-crossing is voluntary – in other cases, forced upon people. We present a series of case studies, drawn from our Australian data, which illustrate the complexity of risk and border-crossing.

3

Risk and Border Crossings

Beck's and others' focus on a broader range of risks – risks of intimate relationships, of work patterns, as well as the environmental risks so graphically displayed at Bhopal and Chernobyl – has potentially opened up attention to an analysis of risk as an aspect of mutable and multiple subjectivities. Yet we find a number of problems with current risk focus.

Most obviously, at the beginning of the twenty-first century, although the issues of genetic engineering, a continuing HIV/AIDS epidemic, public and media fears about GM food, carbon emissions and so on are major practical and ethical agendas for the new century, the criminal risks to human life that have occurred in India, Afghanistan, Palestine, Rwanda, Kosovo and East Timor (to name only the most recent and media-visible) have led to fear, mass migrations, poverty and identity displacements on such a scale as surely to become symptomatic features of what Beck would call 'risk modernity'.

At a slightly less dramatic level, the diaspora associated with other persecutions – of Jews in the Soviet Union, dissidents in South Africa, small businesspeople in South Vietnam, to name only a few – have become a key feature in cosmo-multicultural stories (Hage, 1997) in their new host societies. In Australia, popular multicultural broadcasting channels and genres, the promotion of 'exotic' foods and 'ethnic' inner-city suburbs, the rise of new racist parties, together with tales of invasion ('boat people', 'asylum seekers') and crime (the drug trade associated in Australia with Vietnamese immigrants) are simply some of the circuits of communication which promote the economics of both tourism and risk associated with this massive immigration. Beck's notion of the risk society ignores too much of this. Despite his broader sociology of risk it is too focused on the 'cataclysmic democracy' of publics facing catastrophic environmental hazards to deal adequately with this dimension which is both global and densely local ('glocal') at the same time.

As we pointed out in Chapter 2, lay people see risks as affecting not only their physical being but also their economic status, cultural identity, home 'memory', relationships with others, social standing or status and emotional or psychological states. In the case of migrants to a country like Australia, these risks will be mingled and articulated in complex geographical–biographical and social ways. But, in different ways, so too will others engaged in different kinds of liminal experience, where the margins crossed are borders which are not spatial/geographical, but are temporal (of age), or of sexual practice, or even – as in the case of interviewees reported in this chapter – of knowledge, as new knowledge (about HIV/AIDS) and the deaths of a succession of loved ones makes people realize that they have crossed boundaries of risk, loss and loneliness years before.

We use, in this chapter, the notion of 'border crossings' to illustrate these movements and the risks that may be associated with them. Our use of the term goes beyond the purely spatial/geographical sense of border to examine the meanings of social and cultural borders. We draw here on Douglas' writings on 'Otherness' to theorize border crossings. As we have discussed earlier, Douglas argues that those people or social groups which lie on the borders or boundaries of a society are considered highly risky by those inhabiting the centre. Because of their liminality they are most likely to be constructed as 'Other', as potentially polluting, and thus requiring control and containment. But they are also often regarded as fascinating and attractive because of their very 'Otherness'.

The 'border crossings' of risk that we will discuss in this chapter are of three kinds: immigration and diaspora; sexual preference; and aging. They involve movements across cultural and social borders from the 'knowns' of one's birth country and culture, the dominant and accepted heterosexuality and the privileged youthful body, to the 'unknowns' of a foreign country and culture, a stigmatized homosexuality and an aging body. These movements are associated with risk because of the 'unknown' and the potential state of 'Otherness' they may invoke, but may also be associated with excitement, pleasure or a sense of 'finding' and accepting one's 'real self'.

'Australian' perceptions of risk are the subject matter of this discussion, not to mark off an essentialism (as between 'Australia' in this chapter and 'Britain' later), but rather as a cultural representation. 'Australia' here is the 'lucky country' which still resonates in the minds and the actions of many people here and worldwide. 'Australia' is the land *beyond* the border (the place that exploited peoples try to reach, and older Australians are nostalgic about). But it is also the place *now*, located in a variety of perceptions and practices of risk control and pleasure. It is that liminality – of Australia *there* and *here* as well – that our various case studies of mobility, diaspora, aging, sexuality and knowledge are about.

Narratives of movement

'Australia' has for long been constructed as the narrative closure of other people's 'lack'. The early colonialist target for unruly sons of English gentry had become, by at least the time of early post-World War II, a new home for a 'multicultural' community for economic, political and personal reasons of choice or displacement.

Governmentally Australia presents itself rhetorically as a multicultural society. The paradoxes of having been both a white colonizing and a multicultural 'immigrant' society have, of course, been widely articulated recently within Australia in relation to Aboriginal land rights legislation. Still, Australia continues to be perceived from outside as a relatively safe haven; and as social breakdown and momentous social changes occurred during the early 1990s in Europe (the breakdown of the Soviet Union followed by warring nationalisms, ethnic cleansing etc.) and Africa (the breakdown of apartheid in South Africa followed by continuing poverty and social unrest in that and other African states), Australia continued to attract migrants from these areas. But because of a significant tightening of immigration laws (and an increasing national paranoia about 'asylum seekers'), there has been a strong tendency for only people with middle-class, professional backgrounds to enter. This issue of social class is very evident in our first three risk biographies, of Eric from South Africa, Sasha from the Soviet Union and Rosanna from Spain, all of whom had made the momentous decision as adults to emigrate to Sydney and start new lives.

Eric

As we noted in Chapter 2, a number of our interviewees nominated crossing geographical borders as itself the greatest risk they had taken in their lives. Thus Eric said:

I've moved in my early twenties away from South Africa to England and in my forties from England to Australia. Those were the first two biggest risks I've ever taken in my life. The feeling of nervousness and trepidation and concern and the unknown were just on one level quite fantastic and on the other very scary. And there were catalysts for change that made things either easier or more difficult depending on which opportunity I looked at. But those were the biggest risks I've taken.

It is out of that relationship between determining 'catalysts for change' (lack) and 'nervousness and trepidation' (as the potential of plenitude) that our immigrants' narratives of risk were constructed.

Eric is a 44-year-old university-educated executive officer. He is of English descent, born in South Africa, where, as a youth, he felt at definite risk: 'It was all tied up with the indoctrination that I'd had as a kid and it was a political situation at the time: 1974.' Eric studied Marxist theory at university, which became the catalyst for him leaving South Africa. Through his studies he came to realize the inequities present in his country:

The whole apartheid system, the whole school education system, the whole university education system, everything was geared against the conceptualizing and the recognizing of any left-wing thought, any thought of what you and I would now describe as ordinary behaviour. Any idea that black people in South Africa were disadvantaged, any idea that black people's situation needed to be improved, was seen as being Communist-inspired. It was the external threat. We were happy the way we were, according to the South African government. Any influence to change this was seen as being wrong. Consequently the whole system was geared towards bolstering the status quo. And it took until my final year of university when I took politics, and I was exposed to Marxist concepts and thought and history, that I suddenly realized right, this is it, this is the catalyst, I'm off, goodbye! And I went to England and I joined the anti-apartheid movement.

Thus Eric's self-perceived 'catalyst for change' was Marxism, and he carried this grand narrative with him to Britain, where it instantly encountered another appropriate 'Other': Thatcherism.

However, the early 1980s was also 'historical' for another reason; and it was 'then' and 'there' (in Britain) that Eric crossed another border: that of 'coming out' as gay and beginning his first relationship with another man. Another 'positive' narrative was constructed.

To me it was my 'coming out' relationship, so it was a big experience for me. I felt absolutely in love and absolutely happy, confident and all these sort of things. And it was in London in the early '80s, pre-HIV days, it was '81, '82, '83, and wild times, completely wild. I had a full-time job at the time, I had money, I had income and the risks usually happened after going to a night-club. We'd mix our drinks and drugs, get a taxi, go to a party afterwards. I suppose that the risks that I took were unknown to me at the time, sexual risks for fear of contracting STDs or HIV.

As this account suggests, Eric took many voluntary risks at this time: drink-driving, petty theft when drunk after parties. On one occasion he was chased by two men after leaving a gay bar. But Eric is a very tall, well-built man.

I don't feel I am at risk from crime. I'm fortunate in that I am very tall and very able-bodied and I have a personality [that] is sort of deflective of risks against me when taken in conjunction with my sheer size. I'm six foot two or three, and it's something that I've often thought about, that sheer presence, helped along by size and also helped along by personality.

Eric is reflexively confident about his body; but no less so about his political and gay narratives. What marks his many stories of risk while in London is their sheer number and the exuberance of their telling. A reflexive recognition of this positive lifestyle in addition to his continuing Marxist-influenced narrative is also symptomatic of his Australian stories.

I don't believe that Australians are at great economic risk compared with Africa, compared with countries in south-east Asia, compared with some countries in South America. Compared with the sort of global economy, Australia is not at risk. I think within Australian society though, the biggest threat to stability is happening through the division of society created by extremely unfair and very prejudicial economic systems. They favour rich people and don't favour the disadvan-taged poor people. So I see the biggest risk as a removal of that [typically-Australian] easy-going nature which I've read about. For me it *is* very comfortable, but I'm helped along in that by having a job and living in a nice eastern-suburbs flat close to the beach. So I suppose the risk to society is the increasing inequality, the increasing power and wealth of the 'haves' and the increasing poverty of the 'have nots'.

As we saw in Chapter 2, in concert with many of our other interviewees, issues of class and inequality have by no means fallen off Eric's agenda (as Beck might suppose). Indeed, they dominate it. But they are also interwoven with a range of other (especially lifestyle) risks.

INTERVIEWER: Can you think back to the last time you felt at risk of something?

ERIC: I suppose it was a health risk. It was a fear of HIV infection. There was a test and there was that period of concern while I waited for my results. And there were a few times before then [in] the early 1990s and then again in 1994 or 1995.

INTERVIEWER: So was that due to unsafe sex?

ERIC: Yes. Well, potentially unsafe sex – there are different levels of unsafe sex.

As a health professional, as 'a very cautious person' ('I calculate, I weigh up, I measure, I judge, I procrastinate, I take a long time to decide whether I'm going to do something or not') and as a gay male who has his community's detailed knowledge of 'different levels of unsafe sex', Eric retains a considerable confidence in the face of economic, medical, intimate and lifestyle risks.

> Short-term view I don't feel at risk at all in terms of job security. I feel very positive about the kinds of things I do and the kinds of relationships I have. Health risks? Against some risks I'm insured in terms of health insurance. In other ways, personal behavioural attributes, I don't think I'm at risk from pretty well anything. If I have sex I have safe sex. Crime, no I don't feel under threat.

Risk for this big, professional, middle-class, gay male is both a matter of expert knowledge and the adrenalin of a risky lifestyle. Because, despite Eric's tendency towards 'caution', he has always 'got a buzz' out of risk. Here is a recent example from his rock climbing/bush-walking lifestyle which displays his continuing confidence in his body. He recounts the story of finding himself in a tricky position while climbing near a navy base:

> I've climbed up the cliff face and had to swing myself round on a fence that was between the navy base and freedom. And I was on the navy side and I had to climb over this fence and there was about a hundred foot drop. I was nervous as anything, but I felt comfortable enough in my own physical structure to do that. It was quite nerve-racking though, because it was a rusty old fence. It could have broken. But I took a chance and I was very pleased that I did it, and the fact is I remember it and still talk about it. When I go down there now and I look up, I remember that fence I had to climb. I see it hanging out. It's designed to stop people from going around.

It is this combination of the 'expert' weighing up of the probabilities and the buzz of 'taking a chance' that determine Eric's discursive construction of risk in the interview: 'Taking a risk is very, very necessary, but something which for me requires huge amounts of thought, weighing up all the options and procrastination.'

Compared with victims of displacement, immigrants to Australia like Eric have made what Beck would call a chain of rational arguments and courses of action. These are embedded, as he describes them to us reflexively in the interview, in a series of 'positive/positive' narratives: grand narratives of Marxist theory, of gay pleasures and knowledges, and satisfying memories about his big, male body. But we also found very different 'movement' narratives: 'negative/negative' narratives of fearful and exhausted migrant women; and 'negative/positive' narratives of diaspora, as the next two case studies demonstrate.

Sasha

As was evident from Eric's accounts, knowledge gained through geographical movement can make interviewees especially aware of global similarities and differences. *Diasporic* knowledge, though, is not simply a matter of switching from one culture to another. It is frequently compositely 'balanced' knowledge: knowledge with a foot in two camps, knowledge that aspires to different (even opposing) sets of moralities.

Sasha, a 40-year-old interpreter/translator, came to Australia from Russia in 1991. His personal biography of diaspora thus merges with Russia's momentous transition from the Soviet Union, via glasnost, into Yeltsin's corrupt and economically fraught 'modern' Russia. But Sasha has no experience of this later Russia. *His* Russia is the Soviet Union, and he compares this Russia with his experience of Australia.

There are, he argues, different risks associated with the different cultures. The main social risk in the Soviet Union was the lack of freedom and the democracy he treasures in Australia. The main personal risks associated with this authoritarian regime were associated with the police (one incident concerned drunkenness in the streets after a party) and the army. In the latter case Sasha speaks of the system of conscription and the risk of being killed or brutalized during those years in the military when the Soviet Union was involved in the expansionism (Afghanistan etc.) which helped bring it down. Unlike Eric, Sasha is not a physically strong man. Because he loved to study, and knew that university education was a way of avoiding the army, he followed a tertiary career, and eventually became a university lecturer. In contrast, his brother who was a much tougher character, did army service, was lucky enough to serve in central Asia and survived, though undergoing difficult experiences.

On the other hand, in Australia Sasha now misses many of the 'good things' – the social welfare system and the free education – that were automatic rights in the Soviet Union. Despite the propaganda in the Soviet Union, there was also, he argues, a much more genuine sense of community in Russia than in Australia. 'Solidarity' was not just propaganda. It meant 'real friends and open relationships. Whereas people here [in Australia] are more reserved you know. They don't share as much here, so maybe they're afraid to lose more here'. People in the Soviet Union 'were not spoilt by material possessions, whereas here you could be forgotten quite easily.'

Clearly, Sasha sees a very different set of risks in Australia: to do with individualism, materialism, political corruption (like Eric, he mentions Australian politicians' 'corruption' and 'travel rorts'), and the difficulty for immigrants of starting from scratch. 'In Soviet Union I was not afraid of falling ill, whereas here I try to avoid it at any cost because every day of sickness means loss of income.' As an example, the 'most recent risk situation' he remembers is to do with the cost of having a tooth extraction done. He is forced to suffer the inconvenience and unsightliness of the gap in his mouth because he cannot afford to get the tooth replaced. As a single heterosexual man, he is concerned that his attractiveness to women will be affected: 'So the tooth is not there and I might not have it for several years maybe. It's a small risk of course. [But] it has some implications that affects some [intimate] aspects of my life.' Interestingly, this fear of the costs of health treatment has made Sasha more careful with his body in Australia: he has moderated his alcohol consumption considerably.

Contrasted with these personal biographical risks which Sasha thinks he can manage by careful choices, there are the macro-'western' risks: to do with cloning, genetic engineering, and science and technology which he feels he can do little about.

> I think we're approaching very fast that brave new world described by Huxley. So it's quite real, with advances in science and technology which are quite dangerous for people. And because Australians are so, you know, innovative, they could be the first to face those risks. I just want them to be cautious, to be careful. Not to rush into things.

Sasha is a religious (Jewish) man, and this both moderates and mediates his 'goods' and 'bads' in relation to the different 'risk societies' of the Soviet Union and Australia. In Australia, there is always the chance (unavailable in the Soviet Union) of more discussion of scientific and environmental risks, and thus, potentially, of democratic decisions to change them. 'So I value freedom very much and the responsibility as well.' On the other hand, though, he is very aware of how the

> media is manipulated by strong men, and they don't want people to think. It's entertainment and so much propaganda, not much else. It's all hidden you know, but basically they want idiots, obedient idiots. Particularly when you are in a position of power, then you become a predator, a vulture. And it's all stupid, so I think there should be more discussion in the society, more solidarity, more cooperation. It should be more encouraged so that certain things could be improved and should change.

Sasha feels that men of power and media propaganda are not so different in the Soviet Union and Australia. He hopes that, nevertheless, individuals in Australia can make small changes: 'to do little things, good things in their life which you know, would just make their life and the life of people round them nice.'

However, Sasha is not just a 'spiritual' being. He is also 'unfortunately an ambitious person'.

> There is something inside me which would push me to work and to buy things. Sometimes I want to stop, but I can't. I can stop for a week, or a day, but not for long. And also if you have email then you could communicate with people, if you have a car you can move around and meet many people. Of course, in Australia you could travel overseas as well. So really it's financial, it's social, cultural, if you have money you have better cultural opportunities as well. You can see fine theatrical performances and they are not cheap in Australia. So it's a vicious circle, you know.

47

This is the 'very high emotional price' of taking

> different risks in Australia, so you enjoy your car, you enjoy your computers, email, CDs. I have two computers, I have all sorts of things, but I think financially my life is full of worries. And it's quite serious. It's quite real because banks are quite ruthless you know. And those financial companies, they're ruthless. You don't pay them for two months and they come and repossess everything, whereas in the Soviet Union it was quite different.

This is risk reflexivity, not nostalgia. Sasha is very aware of the good things in Australia. Indeed, if he is nostalgic for anything, it is the 'old' Australia.

> Australia's a wonderful country, a nice place and generally friendly people, and in provinces people are friendlier than in Sydney, while the opportunities are fewer there. But, anyway, there's still, you know, sense of community, and in some neighbourhoods people are not so alienated and they socialize. And also of course there's a lot of freedom on the street compared with many other countries.

This was the 'Australia' that was the plenitude at the end of Sasha's rainbow. But the actuality is different. In his view technological change is bringing an end to this 'pure Australia'.

> The education system has, I think worsened, and instability in some aspects of downsizing and lots of temporary jobs are created. So some people like it, some don't like it. And I sometimes like it, sometimes I don't like it. So there are advantages and disadvantages but of course it's a very sudden and rapid change and sometimes it's not really justified by technology. I think sometimes it's just desire to introduce something new at whatever cost without thinking about human consequences. And also I think that employers now, particularly in large organizations and institutions, not value much their staff so they just sack them and there's not enough recognition for many people. So you're on your own, you know, just surviving the jungle. You have more freedom, of course, but at the same time we're losing the sense of community.

'Freedom' but no 'community'; 'I sometimes like it, sometimes I don't' – Sasha tells us his narratives of diaspora. He is a risk-taker, because 'without those risks you can't move'. Without a risk-taking attitude he would never have given up his stultifying job in the Soviet Union (against all the advice of family and friends), which enabled him, by good fortune, to get part-time university work and thence a regular academic career in Russia. Without a risk-taking attitude he would not have left the Soviet Union either, thus losing that academic career. But 'there are risks in your life every day', and his main strategy in dealing with them is to draw on his own diasporic 'negative/positive' narratives in order to distinguish *culturally* the rationalities of risk.

> You understand what is risky here and what is not. And some Russians who come here of course could do some stupid things because they don't understand the Australian situation, and it's quite acceptable there but it's not here, so it's a risky behaviour here. And vice-versa I suppose, an Australian coming to Russia. So much depends on the cultural and social setting.

Sasha takes care to 'learn about different risks differently', via family upbringing, university education, real life situations, varying life experiences in different cultures. 'With different life experiences sometimes you have to make a mistake in order to learn. So then you understand it's a real risk because before you didn't realize it was a risk.'

Rosanna

Rosanna is 70, a retired cleaner who was born in Spain where she left school early. Her stories of Spain and Australia are nearly all negative.

In Spain, she says, her family came across hard times after enjoying privilege and wealth:

I can remember, my grandfather. He have all town, all deliver, everything was belong to him. My mother was like princess. My grandfather have a casino and lost all in the casino. He have several wives, that's why he have 16 children and all are coming very poor because he lose all in the casino. And then one of his children kill himself because the girlfriend Manuella not have him any more because he was poor. My mother marry the boyfriend, and we are very poor. We hava no house. We hava no clothes. We were not gipsy because we coma from really high, but when you have everything and you lost everything, nobody wanted to know anything. We couldn't pay our rent, we had to live in the street. My mother coming very sick and die from there. No medicine or nothing.

Rosanna goes on to outline the violence she experienced from her brother because of her choice of husband:

My brother nearly kill me. Three, four time he try to kill me because I marry Manuel. I run away to him in middle of the night. [My brother] stabbed my husband. Lucky only it scratch his skin, but all his clothes broken, and I try open the window and [my brother] nearly kill me. So come the police, my brother was in jail for couple of days. And I working very hard, I have to broken the water with a hammer, ice, to wash the baby of my brother's children, and my sister-in-law, and I working so hard.

After emigrating to Australia as a young married woman in search of a better life, Rosanna again encountered harsh conditions and back-breaking work in climatic extremes:

From then I have work all my life, I have been in the asbestos mine and in the north where is very, very hot. I'm ironing for the people clothes and then you are so hot. We're living in the little room like a hut, with the bed like the grass, and the copper one pipe with the water and then the only place we can live in. And it was terrible.

She was then faced with worries about her son's health, followed by difficulties in her relationship with both him and her daughter:

And then from beginning I thinka my son have like the meningitis. For the heat I have to come back six months after. We come back from Perth and my son is already very sick. And from then I hava trouble, I always hava trouble with Paulny. And my daughter Minora is beautiful person, I love her very much, only she's temper, so temper. And she make me cry, really does. But my reason I thought, she one of these like to hurt. Very cruel.

For Rosanna, the current risks she faces concern the continuing problems in her relationship with her children, her son's health and the worsening health of herself and her husband: 'And I always risk it when we are to grow old. Scared very much, very, very much. Oh my health is big mess now. But I worry about my son, think, you know, he's gone worse. My husband is sick too with diabetes.'

Rosanna's life-course narratives have been, it seems, almost entirely around the closed-off risks of a woman exploited both at work and in domesticity in two very different cultures. After all this, still she has few friends and little leisure.

> I tell you I have nothing to do with people. I always my job and my home, my children. Minora said to me many times 'What, do you have no friends?', and I say 'Well, I have your father, I have you, I have my son.' I tell it to everybody. Everybody say 'Hello' to me, very kind, I say to everyone very kind, but I never going very, very close because I hava one friend for 15–16 year, is Spanish, and she's sometime coming home. We have a dinner, we go somewhere or you know, talk. And one day she coming and you know Manuel and Paulny fight very bad, very badly. And from there on she never coming any more.

Perhaps close to the end of her life, Rosanna reflects on it.

> I think through the years Australia past many, many, many terrible jobs, for I work for nearly 27 year now – cleaner in the night time. My husband come and do a little bit. I been working so hard all my life. And they were going pictures, dancing, dinner, and me never. All the while I'm working, keeping the money for the family. If we're improving, I think they give respect, very respect. But I think I should enjoy more my life, and I can be more healthy because I been too hard for myself, and now is too late. Hard to work all time. You think what you can do better. I did wrong in one way, and the other way well, I do better.

As we hear, Rosanna's Spanish and Australian stories have been very negative, and her current impression of Australia is negative also as she observes, and suffers, the crimes of violent young people (including, it seems, her son). Nevertheless, as we also hear, Rosanna is reflexive in her later years, wondering about what 'better' might have meant for her personally, and for her family. She is aware of the way others have made narratives out of her life. 'It feel like my life was all, look if you now want to make a book to sell it, it could be really drama.' But she also believes that her suffering has made her strong, and that it is on this strength that her family depends. This is her central narrative; and Australia is her home. 'If somebody say to me "Are you going to Spain now, you sell everything you have and you going over there and you live there?" And I say "No. No. This is my country and this is where I stay".'

Narratives of sexuality

Our strategy in this chapter has been to focus on dimensions of risk biography that highlight issues of liminality, multiple identity and subjectivity: hence 'border crossings'. This is meant to be a symptomatic rather than representative approach to risk biographies, in so far as we assume all biographies are composed of the 'partial perspectives' of 'insider' and 'situated' knowledges whose 'truths' are contingent on differences of time, space, age, gender, class, sexual preference and other aspects of 'culture' and 'context'.

Moreover our focus first on narratives that are considered in terms of 'lack' and 'plenitude' is not intended to privilege certain terms and concepts within a particular (structuralist) narrative account. These terms were used simply because they seemed appropriate to the common-sense myths about 'leaving here for Australia' which have been circulating in a range of communication forms over many years (any local film festival, for example, would be sure to generate, either seriously or parodically, a number of European films which promote this lack-to-plenitude utopia of 'escaping to Australia').

On the other hand, quite different narrative devices and concepts may be appropriate for analysing other kinds of risk biography, such as those relating to sexual preference. In particular, the very specific time (late '70s/early '80s)/ space (bath house/sauna etc.) co-ordinates of 'coming out' gay sexuality, followed by the terrible knowledge of HIV/AIDS, has made many gay risk biographies into stories of plenitude reduced to lack via the 'truth' of epistemology.

Consider, for example, these two statements by Paul, a 44-year-old Australian-born gay man, who described his own experience of the early 1980s and late 1990s, involving entering the gay community and then living through the deaths of many of his friends and two lovers from HIV/AIDS.

> I think some people still call it coming out, but I find it a quaint 1980s view of life now. But in the early 1980s I 'came out' and once again I used to say to people it felt like being a teenager again, because I realized that by entering the social milieu of the gay community in Sydney in the early '80s was a period of intense sexual experimentation. And although in my mid-twenties, I really was quite naive in terms of the cultures of that particular community. It was an embryonic community in the early '80s, and for several years I was extremely sexually active. And then in 1983 I became aware of this issue HIV/AIDS. And I suppose on reflection now, it's a miracle that I wasn't HIV-infected during that period, because it's clear that HIV was present in Australia from probably 1978 or 1979 onwards.
>
> I've never really been a lonely person in all my life. I'm a very sociable person. But I am starting to find it more difficult to invest energy into renewing relationships. I am in a little bit of an unusual situation, I suppose, because very few men my age would have had such a large number of their social circle die, apart from the classic [case of] the people who lived through the First and Second World Wars ... I have noticed the ill health of a very close friend of mine recently, one of the last surviving HIV-positive friends I have. It has reminded me of my loss as a result of HIV, and that loneliness is something which I think can creep up on you quite easily. It's not something I've had a really strong awareness of early in my life, but I am becoming aware of the dynamic of loneliness as I get older.

In juxtaposition to these two statements, let us now consider two others, one on sexual experimentation in saunas by Murray, a bisexual man, and the second on aging and loneliness by Joan, a heterosexual woman.

> I was at a men's sauna, and I was in a situation where there were several men around me and some of them were actually having sex. And one of the men near me, who was obviously very excited, was trying to enter me I suppose. For want of a better word he was actually trying to fuck me, and he was pushing his penis, well not into me, but onto me. And I felt really in danger from him because he was quite forceful, and he, well he grabbed me and tried to make me do that. I had to push him away. (Murray)
>
> When my husband told me that he was going to leave me [for a much younger woman] I felt at risk. It's a strange risk, but it's a risk of solitude, of being by myself, of being lonely. Yeah, and condemned because I'm older and he'd chosen someone younger. (Joan)

These are very different narratives of sexual danger and loneliness from Paul's story.

For 39-year-old Murray (a university-educated theatre worker), as a bisexual, there are none of the knowledges and certainties about risk and safer-sex that Eric and Paul have gained since the time of their first (early-'80s) encounter with an 'embryonic gay community'. Consequently, their contin-ued sexual experimentation with other men is described very differently. We can contrast Eric's confident talk of dealing with 'potentially unsafe sex. There are different levels of unsafe sex' with Murray's continuing fear.

> Just the fact that somebody is touching me or something, if I don't know them, then just to have someone touching me in a sexual way makes me feel anxious, even though I know there isn't really a risk involved. But I feel at risk at that time, just the anxiety that you can't necessarily totally control the situation, and that there is a small chance that you might contract AIDS and forever regret that, you know. So I suppose I actually avoid those situations for those reasons. Not because I'm terrified about somebody touching me, but because I'm quite seriously scared of somebody's sperm entering my body at some, you know, however it might enter. I'm not actu-ally so scared of getting AIDS so much from a woman, but then I have very little sexual contact with women apart from my regular girlfriend.

Eric and Paul speak of the joys, sensuality and risky exuberance of gay bars and they have confident 'safer sex' knowledge claims via the gay community. Murray on the other hand – who has a regular girlfriend but 'feels a further physical need [for sex with men] that I have to satisfy somehow' – is deeply fearful and uncertain in his sexual relations with other men. He finds them hostile, invasive, dangerous. Although he 'probably would prefer to have casual sex with women, for whatever reason that sort of interaction is unavailable to me, so sometimes I find myself having casual sex with men, and often men I don't know, and some of these men are very dangerous people indeed'. He goes on to describe the bath house experience quoted above. Whereas both Eric and Paul speak critically (from their various Marxist- and gay-informed knowledges) about the media, Murray compares its 'truths' with those he might encounter from his 'dangerous' male pick-ups. 'I trust newspapers, radio more than I trust someone I'm likely to meet on the street or a party or a bus-stop or some place.'

Murray's interview stories come across as epistemologically and socially uncertain: stories of 'dangerous' activities hidden from his regular girlfriend and conducted among shady, aggressively sexual characters whom he must 'push away'. Indeed, Murray gives the impression of reconstructing the 'bisexual as guilty and secret conduit' of AIDS promoted in the popular media (Tulloch, 1992). Murray, like these media representations of bisexuals, casts himself in his stories as a shadowy and (epistemologically) uncertain figure in the public spheres and solidarities of the bath house.

Joan (a 53-year-old homemaker and mature-age student) has a life project. She was brought up in a Catholic household by a very conservative mother: 'she warned me when I was courting, if a boy ever touched me to slap his face. And I had no idea really of where he was going to touch me, or why I had to slap his face.' In response, Joan has deliberately lived the life, where possible, of 'naughty girl'. She described the risks she took deliberately as part of this project of opposition to the 'nice girl' archetype:

Being a girl, you have to take risks at trying to overcome the taboos that [limit] women. Just because I'm a girl doesn't say I can't do it. Yeah, with my riding I used to take risks like jumping a horse over something larger than I thought. I'd take a risk and of course I could do it. I guess smoking my first cigarette was a risk-taking thing and going against my parents' wishes. Probably drinking alcohol, because it's a bit like my boys doing whatever they're doing with drugs. That's a risk because their parents don't want them to. But then, getting married because that was the sort of thing that a country girl did and I didn't have any other option really. I wanted to do it. I'm not quite sure though whether I had a lot of choice in the situation.

It is this life-long project of gender that has recently been threatened by Joan's aging, her own more recent border crossing. The onset of a progressive disease left her quite deaf when she was in her mid-'40s. In addition, her husband has taken up with a much younger woman.

I just thought age would creep up on you gradually and you'd sort of fit into that mould of being older, and you know, you'd comfortably fit into your old chair. But it happened to me far too quickly. I hadn't done all the things that I wanted to do, and I was riding my horses and I couldn't [do that any more]. I suppose when you're 20 you think 40 is old, but of course once you keep going down the line it stretches a bit longer. Anyway, I felt that I didn't want to give up and I still have that, although it's getting harder, but I'm still pushing. I don't want to give up, because I feel that if I sit at home my mind does horrible things to me when I'm by myself, so I keep on pushing.

'Pushing' is directly equated by Joan with gaining more knowledge. She believes, for example, that despite her own recent misfortunes, life generally is getting better: 'It's only three years ago that I had the opportunity to go to university, and perhaps I wouldn't have ten years ago. I'm sure that the education system is more open than it was.' She has a significant belief in 'expert knowledge': when her two younger sons recently told her that they were on speed she sought out all the pamphlets she could find on heroin, speed and other drugs, and left these for the boys to read.

But Joan also values *their* own knowledge. She remembers her own mother's inability to recognize anything but her own perspective. She remembers her own dangerous driving when under the influence of alcohol. Like many parents, she is caught in a tension between responsible surveillance of her children and her belief in the importance of their own age-situated knowledges and perspectives. Even in the case of her husband, she tries to recognize his perspective, and in fact thanks him for having 'taught me most of the sex education I ever had'. In many respects, Joan exemplifies Beck's view that intimate relationships are the site of profound insecurity at the same time as they hold out the promise of ontological security.

I really do feel that he's the partner for me, and I felt that he's taught me an awful lot and I'm very grateful for what he's taught me. But I have a different perspective on our relationship, I think, than he does. I feel a relationship is between two people, where he feels that he's got more to go around and he can share more. And I look around at what's happening in society, and I think that a lot of men have that sort of feeling. To me it's something to do with the way we bring up our boys. It's something to do with truth that boys tend to treat lightly and women don't. I'm not really sure how to explain it. I think I incorrectly said to my boys 'Don't let me see you doing that', which in a way tends to let them say 'OK, if we don't let Mum see us, we can do it'. There's something in the fact that if a woman said she was going to do something she will stick by that usually and do it. Whereas men – I shouldn't generalize I know – but in some cases men tend to think that it doesn't matter so much.

Joan is uncertain, like Beck's subject of risk modernity. But she continually seeks out knowledge – other people's knowledge, expert and lay – as part of her own continuing biography.

If there is a risk that does start to worry me, like when the boys came home and said they were on drugs, if I don't understand that risk, I will then go out and try and learn as much as I can about it. I think that a way of overcoming risk, is to understand what it is that's happening, and if you understand, learn about it, find out as much as you can, then it's probably not going to be a problem.

But learning – expert knowledge – is only part of an experiential life path which helps her adapt to her extremely difficult present circumstances.

Life is [responsible for risk], and changing circumstances. Nothing is meant to be ever the same. You have to be able to adapt to new situations. You can't live your life just in a pattern. I guess my biggest problem when I started off with my life was not realizing that. I just thought that people went through life and you had a sort of pattern you went through, and at this age did that, this age you did this. It just doesn't work like that. In the end you realize that everybody's circumstances are different, and if you can go along with changing circumstances you probably are better able to cope with life than you are hoping that'll all go through a particular pattern.

Joan is still seeking a satisfying relationship based on love between equals, but is aware that she is unlikely to find it, and must find strength in an ability to 'adapt' and not assume a 'particular pattern' for her life. She is highly reflexive about the categories of age (both physical and social) and gender (and elsewhere in her interview she proves to be reflexive about class and race also). Shifting identities, multiple perspectives, a weaving between 'expert' and local knowledges are all ways in which she continues to try to 'overcome the taboos' surrounding women. Despite all, she argues that her present life is 'better, because I'm learning. I can't say I'm going backwards. I've got to say that what I learn each day, what I come up with and confront, is going to make my life. I can only say that what I go through will make me a better person and a stronger person.'

Joan is also reflexively aware of the degree of wish fulfilment in this. But it *is* reflexivity, not fantasy. 'Oh God, I want to be optimistic, but sometimes I think with my life that I, yes, notice I'm being pessimistic. I want to be optimistic. When I'm with myself I'm pessimistic, when I'm with other people I'm optimistic.' Unlike Murray, Joan does find a community – in the 'other people' of her tertiary studies.

In her interview, Joan weaves between medical risks (her sons' and her own), workplace risks (she lost her job as a result of her hearing disability, but replaced it with a university degree course), intimate risks (her husband), and criminal risks (she doesn't think there is more of this than in her childhood – rather it is the way the media report it). Strongly controlling her stories, though, there is an over-riding politics (seeking greater justice) and a strong gender identity (sweeping away the 'particular pattern' imposed by her mother). This is not a woman (despite her very difficult and anxious life) who is lost in post-modernity or, indeed, in the risk society.

The quest for knowledge – epistemologies that will help understand and control risk – has been a key theme of this section on sexual preference and risk. For our last case study of the chapter, we will turn to this theme directly.

Paul is a (university-educated) health-promotion co-ordinator whose liminality resides as much in his knowledge claims as in any of his experiences. He argues that he is:

- 'scientific' in his 'epidemiological relative risk' definition: 'I am a keen observer of the annual reports of the Australian Bureau of Criminology';
- 'social constructionist' in that 'living in a complex industrialized society means that you have a limited capacity to influence some of the major factors which affect your health, your prosperity and your social interactions with other people';
- 'post-modernist' in so far as 'I try to look at the facts as represented by a range of people rather than just one'.

Like many of our interviewees (see Chapter 2), Paul speaks of youthful risk-taking: drink-driving in rural Australia, sexual experimentation etc. Adopting his 'scientific' identity, he compares this with the statistical drop in his risks as an older middle-class male; *except* for the fact that he had 'an unusual life experience' in his mid-'20s: 'in the early-'80s I "came out".' This resulted, prior to knowledge about HIV/AIDS, in an intense period of sexual experimentation. As with Eric, the South African who 'came out' in Thatcher's Britain, this led to a very precise historicizing of Paul's sense of risk. As well as the sense of the 'early-'80s' as a time of unknown risk, there is also a personal (biographical) sense of aging in the context of the AIDS epidemic since then. As Paul recounted in one of the quotations above, living from his 20s into his 40s he became aware for the first time of the potential for loneliness as his friends and partners began to die during the 1990s.

Paul's response to risk is therefore a conjuncture of this detailed historical and biographical moment with a 'social constructionist' sense of history and risk viewed as changing cultural perception. He recognizes that the risks

Australians have faced over the years have changed, but also that their perceptions of risk have changed:

> If I'd been 18 years old [in the 1960s] then there was a risk that I might get conscripted and sent to Vietnam... There was a risk of polio infection in the '40s and '50s to people which medical technology eliminated from my life before it became a great danger to me. So things do change over the years. But there are a lot of things that were happening which were being hidden then, and one of the issues that's been revealed is the pain, the suffering that people faced as a result of family-located and institutionally-located violence. And now people are revealing that they experienced that violence and that pain. Though if you asked people in the '50s and '60s whether that was a risk that Australians faced they would have said 'Oh no! We don't have that problem here.'... So I think risks change, but also the perception of what is happening changes.

This mix of actual historical and perceived historical change in risk behaviour then works itself through each of Paul's areas of risk behaviour: for example in the areas of intimate risks and fear of crime. He feels it is a miracle he was not HIV-infected, and many friends from the period have died. Now he feels he has control of this area: 'I suppose I'm taking a hardened risk-management approach'. He is also aware of the risk to himself of homophobic violence:

> I know that is occurring in the inner city of Sydney, and when I go and socialize in the inner city, if I'm by myself, I am mindful of that danger. I don't submit to it – I will not allow myself. I won't stay at home as a result of that, but I'm alert and I have a prepared set of strategies for dealing with it.

At the same time, however, Paul is also aware that this perception of 'stranger danger' is a specific exception to what is generally a foolishly misplaced fear of crime:

> Really if you look at the statistics, those people, if they're going to be killed, they're going to be killed by a family member or a close acquaintance. And apart from homosexual men, very few people in our society are killed by absolute strangers. This is why I have thought about the issue of homophobic violence because I know that I fit into a category of people in our society who are *genuinely* at risk of being attacked by absolute strangers, and it really dismays me when I hear people going on about, you know, reclaim the night and let's stop paedophilia and all these sort of nebulous issues. I think the worst crime in our society resides within the family. The very unit that people are upholding as some sort of shining ideal, that's the location of some of the most awful abuse that our society understands.

For Paul, in all the areas of risk he perceives, there is this continuous play between his 'scientific-epidemiological' self and his 'social constructionist' self. For instance, in the area of lifestyle risks, he is aware that statistically he is at a greater risk of dying from cancer than HIV/AIDS because of his long years of smoking. But on a daily basis he thinks about the latter not the former. Similarly, in relation to crime risk, his house has been broken into many times in recent years, and, as he says:

> I've never been beaten up on the street, but as I said, I am aware about violence in the inner city where I socialize, and I've had first-hand experience through nursing people who have been

attacked. I have close friends who are nurses now who tell me that they've got yet another hideously disfigured young boy sitting in their hospital having plastic surgery because he had a bottle pushed in his face down at a hotel. So that's the stuff that's real to me and I can respond to it and think, well, has it any personal relevance to me?

There are no economic risks that Paul particularly worries about. He believes that if he lost his job, he could easily get another nursing position. However, again, he emphasizes the broader public's *perception* of risk ('Crime, the increasing ethnic mix, the perception that the world is becoming more complex and the challenge to a homogenous, monocultural myth from the past') rather than changes in risk itself in relation to economic and most other areas of risk. Complexity in the world makes people uneasy, 'particularly those people who traditionally have had a position of privilege simply by virtue of some very superficial characteristics, such as being white, employed, and adhering to a Christian religion'.

Paul does see the 'global risk of becoming an excessively polarized society with increasing differences between the haves and the have nots'. But overall 'I have an optimistic view of life. I acknowledge that our society is becoming more complex. It appears in many ways to be fragmented, however that's not something that particularly concerns me.' For Paul this complexity and what he sees as post-modern fragmentation is a sign of improvement in Australia, rather than greater risk; and he believes that his actual professional activity as a sexual health worker helps open him out to this greater complexity.

A person in my position comes into contact with an enormous cross-section of people. I'm a health care worker and so I'm exposed to the personal viewpoints of hundreds and hundreds of people in a week. And at an academic and professional level I'm also being exposed to lots of different ideas. But if you're living in [a Sydney suburb] and you're working in a factory and you go home and all you do is watch the national television and chill out, then you very easily can get sucked into just seeing the world from just one position.

Concluding comments

This chapter has concerned itself with a number of current themes arising in and from the 'risk society' literature, for example:

- Beck's emphasis that the 'crucial point about the risk society' is the loss of connection between knowledge and decision, between rational arguments and the course of action attempting to resolve dilemmas, between uncertainty and self-control.
- Beck's view that early modernity's naive certainties and claims to human progress have disintegrated as individuals need to seek new certainties.
- The ontological overvaluing in this situation of 'risk modernity' of the 'pure' relationship of intimate love.
- The individualized turning to alternative expertise and knowledge claims.

57

- The issue of the blurring of boundaries between private and public spheres, between socially-everyday and emotionally-intimate, between expert and lay knowledge.
- The negotiation, in this situation, of different sources of knowledge, different circuits of communication, by people differently placed in terms of gender, ethnicity, socio-economic background etc. across a different range of liminal experiences.

Clearly, to have addressed all of these different liminal experiences in this chapter would have been impossible. Hence, our strategy has been to address these issues at the level of the 'situated' and the 'everyday' by way of imposing two 'grids' to our mapping of 'biographies of risk':

1. The different sites of risk: environmental, intimate, lifestyle, health, workplace, economic, criminal; and
2. The different personal and spatial biographies of risk.

Our biographies of risk presented in this chapter have indicated that for many people there are, indeed, very significant uncertainties and a sense of loss of control in the current Australian context. But rather than Beck's 'crucial point' about risk modernity that it depends on a gap between knowledge and decision, many people argue that at the individual level, risk is a tension between rational planning and the 'adrenalin buzz' (and potential outcome) of risk-taking. Even at the broader, societal level where individuals do acknowledge a gap between their knowledge and their actions (for example, in taking financial risks, or in safety at the workplace), familiar modernist 'moral frames' are very often used to explain this gap: the racist propaganda of South Africa's apartheid, the authoritarianism (but also genuine communitarianism) of the Soviet Union, the economic rationalism of Thatcherism and current Australian government policies, the ruthless 'money talks' reduction of the welfare state under current capitalism's 'market' ideology.

Implicitly (and sometimes explicitly) in these biographies of risk, is the call to progress and 'not go back' to an earlier, less fair and equal system. As we saw in the case of Joan, this continued utopian spirit – harried and under assault physically and emotionally though it may be – can be woven through a wide range of risk perceptions across both private and public spheres. But it seems apparent that even while they cross new boundaries and borders (of age, nation and sexual preference, for example), many Australians continue to value the older 'certainties'. This may, of course, be an age factor in itself. Many of our interviewees in this chapter (especially the university-educated ones) were drawing strongly on what they explicitly articulated as '60s/'70s moral frames, even while (in the case of Paul and Murray) talking about the risks of the 1980s and 1990s. And we could certainly draw attention to other biographies of risk – often from younger, less-educated people – which draw much more centrally on television (rather than the university education in the biographies of so many interviewees here) as a major source of risk information. Yet even here, the perceptions are neither 'late modern' nor 'postmodern' but often rather 'old' and monological: 'ethnics' are seen to threaten Australian workers with unemployment, 'paedophiles' are bogeymen outside, not inside, the domestic space.

We have seen cases where the 'pure' relationship of intimacy (Giddens, 1992) *is* sought as a place of ontological security. But at the same time we have seen (even in those cases sometimes) a valuing of multi-perspectivism that is embedded in modernist beliefs. In Joan's case, this was the result of a determinedly situated perspective, in seeking to understand her children and partner in terms of their own values in the context of (and sometimes against) her own interests. In the case of the highly educated Paul, this multi-perspectivism was articulated as a new postmodernism. But he, too, retains a strong space for the epidemiologically 'real'; as well as a 'social constructivism' which is all about real structures of power, corporatism and globalization. He also (in discussing criminal risk) has a strong sense of the risks of homosexual bashings, rather than the many break-ins he has encountered, the latter verbalized through other professional circuits of communication within the hospital setting.

Very few of our interviewees, indeed, seek alternative expertise and knowledge claims (although no doubt a larger sample would reveal both many new-ageists and Beck's organized 'new politics' groups). Rather, nearly all of them opted for a judicious blending of their own 'experience' or 'intuition' (nearly always rated 'most trustworthy source of risk information') with the opinions of family, friends who had had similar experiences, doctors, financial advisers and other traditional experts. The failure of experts was not in fact emphasized, and when these were mentioned this tended to be at the societal level: governments, politicians, occasionally corporate leaders. Rather, as in Chapter 2, most people felt that they themselves were responsible in some way for most of their risks, and most also believed that, without risk-taking, life could not proceed or be of much value.

Our empirical focus on several different 'borders' of risk allowed us to observe *both* the blurring of boundaries between private and public spheres (and between socially-everyday and emotionally-intimate risks), *and also* their situated, localized negotiation. Joan's social biography as a woman who refused her citation as 'young girl' by her mother was – or had to be – worked through a range of recent risks in relation to her aging, her parenting of teenage boys, and her marriage to a sexually-erring husband. Alternatively, localized fears of risk (as in the case of Paul's fear of bashing) were embedded in broader societal knowledge (about the misconceived emphasis on 'stranger danger', or about the increasing 'dichotomizing' of the 'Other' in Australian society).

As we observed in Chapter 2, overall in Australia there seems to be much less concern with the risks that Beck foregrounds: the scientifically-based failures or uncertainties surrounding environmental catastrophes, human genetics, cloning or genetically modified food. But then Australia has neither had its Chernobyl, nor has this traditionally beef-eating community suffered Britain's BSE crisis. Each of these events was deeply symbolic as well as actual: Chernobyl as constructed in the American media as a Soviet rather than a nuclear risk (see Allan, Adam and Carter, 2000), and BSE as a media crisis of national identity (Brooks and Holbrook, 1998). In the next chapter we begin our focus on the British interview data, with a discussion of some case studies from Oxford.

4

Individualization, Risk Modernity and Biography: The Case of Work

Everything ... becomes an integral component of the individual biography: family and wage labour, education and employment, administration and the transport system, consumption, pedagogy, and so on ... What is demanded is a vigorous model of everyday life, which puts the ego at its centre ... and permits it in this manner to work through the emerging possibilities of decision and arrangement with respect to one's own biography in a meaningful way. (Beck, 1992: 136)

Beck's integral text *Risk Society: Towards a New Modernity* (1992), includes many observations on the nature of employment in the evolving risk society. Key to his analysis of employment are the concepts of reflexivity and individualization, which also underpin his assertions on other aspects of subjectivity and social relations. As we noted in Chapter 1, for Beck, reflexivity is a key outcome of late modernity. The concept of individualization is perhaps even more important in Beck's analysis of the labour market. Individualization, as we discussed in that chapter, involves the breaking down of traditional patterns of behaviour and expectations, again as an outcome of modernization. As a result, people cannot rely upon the old categories of social class, family relationships, gender, nationality and so on to structure their lives and provide security. Instead, they must constantly make decisions in the face of a number of choices with potentially disastrous outcomes.

Beck sees individualization as taking place under the familiar signs of capitalist media organization, commoditization and consumption:

The forms of existence that arise are the isolated mass market, not conscious of itself, and mass consumption of generically designed housing, furnishings, articles of daily use, as well as opinions, habits, attitudes and lifestyles launched and adopted through the mass media. In other words, individualization delivers people over to an external control and standardization that was unknown in the enclaves of familial and feudal subcultures. (Beck, 1992: 105, 132)

In such comments Beck emphasizes the *continuation* of industrial (capitalist) systems: for example in his remarks about the world television audience consuming institutionally produced television programmes from Honolulu to Moscow to Singapore, a global standardization via which 'television programmes arrange in one stroke both the daily and the weekly schedule of the family' (1992: 133).

Individualization, therefore, is far from being a personalized, privatized or solipsistic pattern. Rather, the

> private sphere is not what it appears to be: a sphere separated from the environment. It is the outside turned inside and made private, of conditions and decisions made elsewhere, in the television networks, the educational system, in firms, or the labour market, or in the transportation system, with general disregard of their private, biographical consequences. (1992: 133).

In relation to the labour market, a growing flexibility of working hours and the progressive decentralization of the work site have led to greater uncertainty and new social problems. Chief among the latter is what Beck terms 'new types of flexible, pluralized underemployment' (1992: 129), which in turn create 'new types of life situations and biographical developmental patterns' (1992: 130). The 'invisible' and uncertain qualities of the new work order have been determined by microelectronics' de-standardization of labour. Beginning with electronic automation of automobile, chemical and machine tool industries:

> After a long period of accustomization, it has come to be taken for granted in industrial society that wage labour is to be performed outside the home ... merged in the future into a new system of flexible, plural, risky forms of under-employment ... The place of the visible character of work, concentrated in factory halls and tall buildings, is taken by an invisible organization of the firm. The observable symptom of such a transition would be the gradual abandonment of large-scale work buildings ... If one considers these consequences of the de-standardization of working hours and work locations in their totality, then one can say that a transition is occurring in industrial society from a uniform system of life-long full-time work organized in a single industrial location, with the radical alternative of unemployment, to a risk-fraught system of flexible, pluralized, decentralized underemployment. (Beck, 1992: 144, 142, 143)

Beck sees industrial (capitalist) society and risk society continuing side-by-side, at least at the moment. Certainly, 'a new division of the labour market is created between a uniform standard industrial society labour market and a flexible, plural risk society for underemployment, where the second market is quantitatively expanding and increasingly dominating the first' (1992: 144–5). But he argues that this 'future system of pluralized, flexible decentralized underemployment occurs under an unchanged logic of profit-oriented rationalization' (1992: 149).

For Beck, the 'risks accompanying ... underemployment [which] compete with the partial freedom and sovereignty gained [by employees] in being able to arrange their own lives' (1992: 148) are not clearly managed and mobilized by solidarity groups. Instead, the uncertainty of work risks must be managed by another central development of risk society: the risk biographies of individualization. Beck argues that many of the organizing and identity-giving features of industrial modernity – the family (with the women's role ordained as 'home support'), the factory (promoting class visibility and consciousness), and permanent employment (as career narrative) – begin to disintegrate in late modernity. The factory (or concentrated workplace) and the career narrative are fragmented by new technologies and under-employment.

The family unit is put under threat as the market dictates mobility rights across its membership.

In the absence of traditional support relationships and commitments, people become more dependent on the labour market to construct their biographical patterns: 'Wage labour and an occupation have become the axis of living in the industrial age' (Beck, 1992: 139). People are therefore more dependent on the vagaries of economic cycles and market, but have very little control over them. Indeed, Beck goes so far as to claim that 'individualization delivers people over to an external control and standardization that was unknown in the enclaves of familial and feudal subcultures' (1992: 132).

While individualization tends to represent the individual's biography as self-constructed, Beck also emphasizes the new solidarity groupings that signify the risk society. 'It may be incidents such as the planned highway in the vicinity of one's own back yard, the worsening school situation for children or the atomic waste storage dump being built nearby which cause aspects of a "collective fate" to penetrate into consciousness' (1992: 134). But when the new sub-politics of resistance do not relate to risk society's 'immiseration through fear' – when, particularly, it relates to 'the isolated mass market, not conscious of itself, and mass consumption of generically designed housing, furnishings, articles of daily use' – then Beck seems far less sure about a new sub-politics of resistance. These perceptions of 'collective fate' in Beck's thesis become localized, pluralized, eclectic and deeply embedded in personal biographies. Crucially, for Beck the 'connections and fractures' generated by institutional systems 'continually produce frictions, disharmonies and contradictions within and among individual biographies' (1992: 137). Risk biographies become the only map available in everyday life, as the individualized citizen chooses between daily knowledges, and much less often it seems, between social (sub-political) affiliations.

There is, thus, a deep 'hybridity' within Beck's own thesis: between the 'new' public sphere of 'afraid' citizens, and his privatized 'model of everyday life, which puts the ego at its centre'. It is in this *latter* sphere that '"capital" disappears as the binarized cause of immiseration' and 'it is much more likely [that] events are considered "personal failure".' Yet, as Beck says, the construction of risk biographies as the necessary (and only remaining) agency means that risks are perceived as interwoven into the life course, and as interconnected rather than separated across different boundaries: 'Everything ... becomes an integral component of the individual biography: family and wage labour, education and employment, administration and the transport system, consumption, pedagogy, and so on' (1992: 136).

Some recent research by social geographers has begun to critique and use Beck's work to research contemporary labour market issues. For example, Ekinsmyth has drawn attention to the gaps that need to be filled in Beck's risk society thesis in relation to the labour market. She argues that '[k]ey amongst these is an adequate conceptualization of power, especially with

63

respect to the power of capital *viz a viz* the agency of workers, the role of geography, especially the local; and the role of axes of social differentiation in an area where they yet prevail' (2000: 2–3). Similarly, power in the risk society is a central focus of Butz and Leslie's examination of General Motors automobile manufacturing, where: 'Corporate strategies ... creat[e] ... a terrain of anxiety emanating from the macro-scale [which] operates on individual bodies, and places them within a larger set of interactions with other bodies elsewhere' (2000: 9).

As we pointed out in Chapter 1, the risk society thesis in general has been frequently criticized for its meta-theoretical focus, lack of empirical engagement and inattention to the fine quotidian detail of how people engage with concerns about risk as part of their everyday lives. At least one critic (Miller, 1999) has claimed that the grand theory approach taken by Beck in fact precludes the testing of his theories about risk and late modernity by using empirical research. Miller quotes C. Wright Mills in his criticism of Beck: 'The basic cause of grand theory is the initial choice of a level of thinking so general that its practitioners cannot logically get down to observation ... This in turn is revealed as a partially organized abdication of the effort to describe and explain human conduct' (Mills quoted in Miller, 1999: 1251). This charge – that Beck and his followers *cannot logically* get down to observation – will be questioned here. It is a serious charge, but not one shared by all commentators. Ekinsmyth, for example, also notes Beck's tendency to meta-theory and the need for empirical interrogation. But she sees the theory's generality as its strength, in providing

> a necessary correction to the narrow and compartmentalizing theory that has dominated some spheres of social scientific endeavour ... in more grounded writings about the changing nature of society, economy and polity. Shifting and contradictory positions are instead the under-pinnings of the risk society ... [E]xploration of ambiguity in a specific empirical industrial context can be revealing. (2000: 2)

At the same time, however, Ekinsmyth uses her own detailed empirical research to critique the risk society thesis for its failure to adequately engage with power. She asserts that:

> Contained within the thesis is powerful allusion to the constraining structures that limit individual freedom and choice in the risk society, but there is little attempt to theorize what these might be or how they might operate ... Similarly the risk society framework ... can be criticized for its ... under-theorization of the role of traditional axes of social differentiation ... In so far as these continue, the opportunities for self-management of life biographies for many remain limited. (2000: 19–20)

In contrast, Butz and Leslie *assume* in Beck what Ekinsmyth senses only as 'powerful allusion', and so extrapolate directly from his risk society framework to extend it within a strongly materialist epistemology. Thus they map the risk perceptions of Canadian automobile industry workers across 'three geographic scales': the global, the local and the temporal/spatial configurations of work-risk on the body. They extend the risk society debate empirically in four ways:

1. By moving empirical employment research on from its preoccupation with the service sector to the manufacturing sector;
2. By drawing on Beck's observations on the new 'invisible organization' of the firm to examine the increasing perception of risk by workers faced with the 'boundary-crossing and boundary-changing potential' (2000: 5) of globalized capitalist industries;
3. By demonstrating that these boundary-crossing tendencies (operating in this case within the one manufacturing site) lead to increased – but much less determinate or officially recognized – risks of bodily injury;
4. By focusing on Beck's emphasis on the subjectification of risk to give 'careful attention to the experiences and discourses through which workers are subjected to risk, and through which they respond' (2000: 5).

As with Ekinsmyth's analysis, there is never any doubt where power lies. It resides with capital – and Butz and Leslie demonstrate the way in which transnational corporations mobilize the various spaces (global, local and embodied) via which 'capital searches for more profitable sites of accumulation' (2000: 8). But (again as in Ekinsmyth's account) Butz and Leslie find the risk society thesis' emphasis on the perceived invisibility, incalculability and ambiguity of risk, choice and constraint to be valuable conceptual stimulants for further empirical thinking about agency and power in everyday life.

The problematic nature of calculability in the risk society is, as we noted above, one of Beck's most foundational themes. It is clear that it is the geographers' focus on incalculability in new forms of employability and the mapping of this risk across changing time/space coordinates which enables them to find the risk society thesis so rewarding as a basis for empirical/theoretical work. A traditional *political economy* – of globalized capitalist accumulation – is never far from the centre of their analysis. Ekinsmyth is easily able to illustrate Beck's underlying emphasis that 'do it yourself biographies' are 'thoroughly dependent on the market society' (2000: 6). Butz and Leslie's 'extension' of Beck also clearly indicates the continuing class parameters of risk. And Ekinsmyth relates the new risks of under-employment to categories of gender, age and class (noting that Beck does not do so in any great detail). In each case, however, the empirical case study draws powerfully off the 'invisibility' and 'ambiguity' valencies of Beck's work, to then re-embed them within 'modernist' categories of capital, class and gender. The blurring of boundaries, the loss of rooted and experienced *place* in the face of new transnational space leads to a loss of ability to calculate, predict and control on the part of the workers. Thus risk society's 'incalculability' enters biography in a meaningful way.

We would argue that Beck could certainly not be accused, in principle, of omitting the importance in his theory of the 'everyday' and its situated, local negotiation. Indeed, he argues for the importance of focusing attention on how individualization 'can be understood as a change of life situations and biographical patterns' (1992: 128). What he can be criticized for, though, is

65

allowing the individual-everyday to drop out of both his theory and his (lack of empirical) method except as monological categories (interest groups, etc.) within his theory of a new sub-politics. It is not in the 'middle-level' areas of industrial conflict and change that Beck's theory of risk society needs modifying (though it certainly needs extending empirically). Rather, what is most needed in revision of Beck's theory is analyses of the ways in which reflexivity and individualization are experienced as part of personal biographies and how they are structured via such categories as class and gender.

'Traditional' versus 'high tech': some Oxford case studies

We suggested above that it is at the everyday 'risk biography' rather than the 'new sub-politics' level that Beck's theory of power, discourse and agency is weak. We were interested in Beck's notion of a new division of the labour market as between a standard industrial 'visible' location and the flexible, plural risk society of 'underemployment'. How would the risk perceptions of these differ? A discussion of two traditional 'industrial' workers and two 'high tech' workers from our Oxfordshire interviewees will illustrate our approach.

Ian and Keith

Ian is one of the Rover (Cowley) car workers we talked with in Oxford, interviewed the day that news broke about BMW pulling out of Rover. He is 37, has completed trade qualifications, and joined Rover 20 years ago as a tool fitter. Cars (as with many British interviewees) are a major focus of his risk concerns: for his own safety (he takes time in the interview to elaborate about one Cowley roundabout he fears driving through); his children's safety (he has chosen to live in a suburban close to protect them from through traffic); fear of crime and so on. However, unlike most other British or Australian people we interviewed, cars are also Ian's economic lifeblood, and have been the cause of his 'upward mobility' reflexive narrative, taking him from his council estate working-class childhood to a 'nice house' and a 'prospered life style'. As with many of our other interviewees, this development has also led to a reduced fear of crime on Ian's part (the immersion of young people in the drug economy and fear for one's children in this context – even in the favoured Oxfordshire villages that surround the city – was a persistent theme in our interviews).

But on the day of the interview Ian is facing the BMW closure announcement, and observes that 'whether there is a job for me in engineering I have yet to find out'. To 'find out' more on this day, he is using the works' Internet (where changing bulletins are posted) and listening to the local radio, which is carrying the breaking news by the hour. But otherwise, 'finding out' depends at this stage on 'common talk' whose source is very distant from his own everyday context:

> Well, will they carry on in this country producing at the Cowley plant? I am under the impression now that it is just going to be used for manufacturing of the new Mini and there is talk of Land Rover coming down here because the Land Rover has been sold as well. I haven't got a clue, to tell you the truth at the moment.

Lack of control over this 'talk' doesn't mean he is lacking local knowledge as to the reasons for this closure announcement:

> Rover's problems I blame, well partly down to the management, partly down to the government, I mean it is been going on for years ... Since the sort of first month when I started 20 years ago it was going to shut. I have been there 20 years and perhaps it will come true now, I don't know. But years of under investment etc., etc. and bad management, it has all accumulated. BMW took us over in 1994 and they sort of stood back for a few years, and it is only the last couple of years that we have met German people. I think they have finally realized there is no chance, and that is why they have sold it all off today. They have kept just Cowley at the moment. Yes, Cowley is up-to-date and Longbridge has been left out of any investment by BMW because I believe they have that in mind all along to do this. They did invest in Cowley quite heavily over the last four to five years, in that they re-developed it in effect.

Ian is very aware, as Butz and Leslie emphasize, that '[i]f space is the terrain in which capital searches for more profitable sites of accumulation, then place represents the rootedness of labour' (2000: 8). Like the Canadian General Motors workers they interviewed, he is placing his hopes – in the midst of uncertainty – on the 'boundary-crossing and boundary-changing potential' (Butz and Leslie, 2000: 5) of the globalized BMW company as it (perhaps) re-draws its British map around Cowley, not Longbridge.

Keith, 47, another Cowley Rover interviewee, tells a similar tale. He also indicates how proactive a skilled worker can be in trying to negotiate a career in the context of 'common talk' about employment risk – but also how, as Butz and Leslie show, manufacturing workers are ultimately subject to 'invisible' forces in a globalized economy. Keith has worked at Rover for 32 years, and from the time he finished his engineering apprenticeship and moved into the toolroom, people had been rumouring about risk of closure. Like Ian, he closely observed patterns of investment at different Rover sites. Recognizing that of the two Rover toolrooms at that time more investment was going into the Swindon one, he had 'decided to do something different at Rover'. Even though he 'loved his toolroom job', he had moved into the drawing office, after taking advice from a couple of men who had already done so: 'That was a big risk for me because it was a whole new ball game. We had to take a pay cut to do it, all six of us, and it turned out to be the best move I made in my life and in my career really.' Subsequently (just two years prior to the interview), the Cowley toolroom had been closed.

Like Butz and Leslie's General Motors workers, Keith now experienced the fact that employees could do a good job, and the plant still be closed because of larger corporate imperatives, and this was heightening his sense of unpredictability in the present crisis. 'BMW then decided they would send all the work out to other companies to do the toolroom, so because of that there were no requirements for toolmakers.' He noted (like the General

Motors workers) how this had had a demoralizing effect on the former toolroom workers:

> Throughout all of Rover there are no toolrooms and that put a highly skilled group of individuals onto the track or they left, and most of them have gone on the production lines. There was a cut in money and it was also demeaning to them. It's not demeaning being a production worker, but when you are a timed-served person and that is the only job they can find for you, that is called demeaning. I think, to be truthful, they are putting their health at risk by doing what they are doing by being down there because that is a very demoralizing and very depressing.

As with Butz and Leslie's car workers, the subjectification of risk becomes an important part of Ian's and Keith's risk narratives. But so too is 'glocal' discourse. Both Ian and Keith have been at Rover long enough to observe the process of concentration and globalization. As Keith tells us:

> I mean, in our own case we were sold by the government to British Aerospace and all British Aerospace did was asset-strip us, and then they sold us on again. They made a huge profit out of doing nothing, no investment at all, just asset-stripped and you can see that happening not just in England but all over the world. You can see it, not just in the manufacturing industry, you can see it all other industries and being in insurance and what have you, they are all becoming bigger and bigger, and what happens is that as soon as they do that, they cast off people all the time.

This has deeply affected their sense of citizenship. Both Ian and Keith feel very betrayed by British governments. Indeed, Ian waited for the interview to conclude before asking for the tape to be switched back on to vociferously blame the Thatcher government for the destruction of the manufacturing base, which in his view has had long-term consequences in relation to the current problems with the motor industry. Keith is also bitter about both the government and the British media. He argues that the media

> can start rumours and can force people's way of thinking of that. They can be very critical of a vehicle and that can kill it, that will stop people from buying it. If you get anything wrong with one vehicle, if it is a fault, for instance, they then put a recall on some of their vehicles, and it is not a problem. But if say a *Rover* gets recalled for anything, then [the media advertise that as] typically Rover's lack of foresight and bad engineering.

Both these Rover workers have considerable experiential knowledge of the economic risks of globalization, but no access to decision-making areas that put them and their families at risk. This aspect of their everyday life is out of control in a way that other areas are not – where, as Ian says, 'you try and go by the rules of the road and rules of life in general. You know that by changing a plug, you know what has got to be done'. Both are fully aware of what Beck calls the new risk economy, 'opening up of *possibilities to choose* (for instance, diverging professional mobility of the spouses ...)'. As Keith says, if the Rover plant closes he will have to sell the house which they bought as 'a shell', and in which they invested all their savings to rebuild it, to be (like Ian) in a safer area. 'The field I work in I would more likely have to go abroad to get employment, and that would mean splitting the family up if they didn't come with me. My daughter works now, so it would mean splitting the family, so I find that a quite frightening risk actually.'

In the area of globalization and risk, both these men have considerable knowledge – but the defining 'talk' is always elsewhere. In the area of *environmental* risk, however, another set of knowledge relations applies. In this case it is not that Ian has knowledge, but no power of access to policy discourse. Rather, here he believes he has no knowledge at all, and the man who feels betrayed by government as a citizen at work, conforms to (and trusts) his government's risk regulations. Asked about the risks of GM food, he says:

> Well to tell you the truth I don't really understand what it is all about. I don't really worry about what I eat, actually. I don't know what the danger is of genetically modified tomatoes or what have you. I don't know whether there was one about genetically modified tomatoes, but I have heard about it on the news. And also at work there is Cornish pasties that have been genetically modified substances in them. No, call me ignorant or what have you, I don't know the dangers of a genetically modified Cornish pastie! The way I look at it is, if it is on sale to the public to eat then it must be all right. I would trust the safety standards of the foods, the government regulations office, because as I said, I can't understand what the problems with them are, because obviously food poisoning is a problem with any food.

For some years BMW's 'German people' were as 'invisible' (to use Beck's concept) to Ian as the risks of the GM tomato or Cornish pastie. And as Beck might predict (via his analysis of risk-knowledge and class), this industrial worker puts his trust, in the latter case, in government scientists and inspectors. This is not a level of 'incalculability', in that Ian sees no particular difference between the GM issue and any case of standard 'food poisoning'. The difference – given his lack of access to decision making in both areas – lies in his trust in governments in one area of risk and not in another.

'Incalculability' in Ian's risk biography is not too much of a factor in his domestic life either, except in its relationship to the 'border-crossings' of economic globalization. There the invisibility of the 'German people' related to an area of knowledgbility where Ian (like Keith) was already well-versed, wanted to know more about, and was denied, even up to the day of the interview. Here knowledge and power were *seen* as integrally related, and citizenship denied because knowledge was denied. In relation to science and environmental issues, however, Ian was not worried about 'invisibility', and felt it no more subjectively 'demeaning' (Keith's word) than requiring an expert to check up on the risks of food poisoning. Clearly, here, there was no new sense of solidarity of Beck's kind in the face of global 'catastrophe'. But nor too (again as Beck would predict) was there any talk of class or union solidarity in the face of BMW. Ian spans – with double powerlessness – the 'overlap' of industrial and risk modernities.

The kind of solidarity these men did draw on, however, is illustrated more clearly in Keith's case. His response to the GM issue was different from Ian's. Keith's experience with big business, and his disappointment over the government's handling of Rover has carried over more consistently into his attitude to GM food. Like Ian, he has read newspapers and watched television documentaries about it and comments

I am dead against it. I would tend to believe the people against it, like Greenpeace or any written work that has been in the papers I have looked at. I certainly don't believe the politicians and I certainly don't believe big business because they are promoting it, and the only reason they are promoting it is the money. I don't think anything should be done until the proper studies are actually proven that it is either a good thing or bad thing. I still don't believe in genetically modifying anything.

Keith has lost his trust in big corporations and government even more than Ian has. But both Rover workers find their solidarity very centrally in their family and in the consuming patterns (houses, cars and so on) that will keep them healthy and safe. For Keith, moving to a 'nice area' of Oxford has meant 'better hospitals and schools', as well as less fear of crime. Despite Beck's view on the disintegrating importance of the family as a structuring institution, the family has remained a 'solidarity' structure among manufacturing workers when few others could be found. Keith (who may soon be making the decision about whether to go abroad to work) went out of his way to conclude the interview as follows: 'The only thing I can say and recommend is that in most cases when you make a decision you shouldn't make that decision on your own; you should make it with family, so that you get a more balanced perspective of what you are trying to do.'

Beck's 'invisibility, incalculability and ambiguity of risk' certainly exists for these manufacturing workers. But Beck needs to differentiate his different kinds of 'invisibility', within the different time/space co-ordinates of corporate 'border-crossings' (the 'German people'), and in relation to different everyday senses of knowledge, expertise and citizenship (Ian's GM-labelled Cornish pastie versus his use of the firm's Internet to find out more about BMW).

Especially because of the importance of family solidarity in the face of corporate-enforced divisiveness at work (Cowley *v* Longbridge, Cowley *v* Swindon) or as British citizens, *threats* to the family (whether economic, educational or criminal) were major worries among these workers. Keith's current concern about losing his Rover job was *both* that he would lose his family contact *and* that (because of diminishing house prices as a result of a whole population out of work) his family would be driven out to live in some less safe area.

In this context, another former Rover worker we interviewed emphasized very clearly the important fear of crime aspect which is almost entirely missing from Beck's risk society:

I think I control my own environment, my own house. I worked in industry, I worked on maintenance and I am quite capable of handling anything that goes wrong in my own house, whether it be electrical, water or gas or anything, I can handle that myself, I don't worry about that. Crime I have no control over that at all, I have no input or control, nothing.

This former Rover worker retired with a pension before the closure, so his 'big picture' fear is less to do with BMW than Ian's or Keith's. But he does have a big picture fear: fear of crime, as also do Ian and Keith. Lack of control – over work, then over housing, then over fear of crime – ran like a narrative thread through many of these 'traditional' workers' risk biographies. This, far more than environmental issues and biotechnology, created their 'risk society'. And so for these manufacturing workers, distribution conflicts (symptomatic of Beck's 'industrial modernity') were *generated*, rather than being replaced by, risk conflicts.

Isobel

We can compare the negotiation by these Rover car workers of risk related to their employment with that of Isobel, 33, who has her own IT company in Oxfordshire. She is a scientist who has invested in an MBA and started her business part-time.

Like Ian, when asked to define risk Isobel focuses immediately on economic and financial risk. 'To me the first meaning of it is to do with business, after that it is do with finance, and thirdly it might be personal risk.' But unlike Ian and Keith, she feels she has all these areas of risk under her control:

Again, what is major financial risk? You see to some people, being ten thousand pounds in debt is a big scary thing. I have been at least that much in debt, not including a mortgage. And I don't regard that as particularly scary, because as long as you can see where the future pay off is, as long as you can always see that there is going to be one, and your circumstances are going to improve such that you are not over stretching yourself, then you accept it and say 'Okay, this is a calculated risk, I have calculated the odds.' But you don't sit and be in fear. The worst thing that can happen is that we don't get anywhere, and we have to abandon and go and get jobs – oh dear! That wouldn't be financially too terrible. I am not scared of business risks at all. We have chosen.

Isobel feels quite capable of moving backward and forward between 'flexible' and 'inflexible' employment, in Beck's terms; as well as between full-time and 'risky underemployment'. She defines herself (and her husband, who also has a business) as 'ahead of the field' in two important respects. The first is in terms of her 'high tech' competencies, in comparison to people like Ian and Keith:

I think [there is] less risk of just about every kind for somebody who is educated and computer literate, almost to the point where I have a hard time seeing how you would even worry about having a job. But if you think a job is going somewhere to work, where you take a bus, or bike or drive, near to your home, stay there until 5 o'clock and then come home, if that is what you think a job is then, yes, I think that is going to change. But if you think a job is working a certain number of hours a week and getting paid for it, it doesn't matter where you work, it doesn't matter exactly what you do, it doesn't matter how you deliver your work, then I think those kind of jobs, that kind of opportunity is just increasing.

Clearly Isobel, like most of the other 'high tech' business people we interviewed in Oxfordshire, is very comfortable indeed in Beck's new 'invisible' employment: without factory walls, without Ian's risky drive to work, without Keith's feared-for 'job for life'. As Beck would predict, the concept of a 'job for life' was a central one for very many of our interviewees; and it was the 'new technology' rather than the 'traditional' workers who recognized its passing with equanimity. Again and again among the high tech interviewees we heard Isobel's comment about having the 'skills to get another job anywhere'; and among many of the women this confidence was (as Beck would also predict) blended with a part-time occupation that gave them time for child care.

The second area where Isobel felt 'ahead' was as an entrepreneur, particularly in relation to the banks and government. If it were not for government and bank regulation, Isobel believes she and her husband would take more financial risks, and argues that 'there is too much intervention. People should be allowed to take more risks if they want.'

> The banks are so careful, they will not lend you money if they think you are not going to be able to pay it back. We would be happy to take a bigger risk than the bank would let us, let's put it that way. The bank is what stops us. We found that to be a bad thing. Business is not like science where there is one or two ways to do something. There are so many different ways to do something in business. You have to spend a long time thinking and be more creative. But I have to say the banks take a very sober attitude to risk. They are safety-Nazis.

In fact, Isobel reasons that her own personal areas of risk-taking are directly related to this over-provision of social and economic safety nets. Her most recent risky experience was during 'aggressive downhill skiing' with her daughter, and she argues that people do this kind of thing *because* of the safety nets elsewhere:

> It is extreme sports probably where people are taking their risk now. You have to wonder why are extreme sports so popular nowadays, when they weren't ten years ago? It is because there is not enough risk in ordinary life. So people have to compensate by climbing mountains and bungy jumping.

For Isobel, risk-taking is *the* defining aspect of the 'human condition', and so she must find it somewhere:

> I think risk and pain and misery are all parts of existence, and they are part of what make us become impelled to success. If we lived in a garden of paradise, we would still be there, munching on food and saying, 'Oh this is quite nice really, we don't need any more'. It is only the presence of any kind of adverse possibility that affects anything, that makes you want to improve your situation.

Thus, although she is aware that profound economic changes threaten some people with unemployment, she believes in the power of new technology and private enterprise to resolve the problem for most of them. In every aspect of her life, Isobel feels in control of risk. She wouldn't go alone at night to certain areas of Oxford (including the area of the Cowley car works), but she doesn't want to anyway. She would like to smoke, but chooses not to because of her awareness of cancer risk (which is particularly acute because some members of her family died of this disease):

> For instance, I would never smoke, and I actually would quite like to because I quite like the smell and the taste. But to my family that is practically a suicide letter, because of such high

incidents in it of cardiovascular disease. I know it would be just an unbelievably stupid risk, tantamount to taking 10 or 20 years off my life at will. So I wouldn't take that kind of risk.

Here, personal and scientific knowledges intersect. As a microbiologist, Isobel knows about cancer scientifically, as well as ·experientially via her family history. But whereas Ian is a hybrid citizen (trusting the government in relationship to food and environmental risk, but losing faith in it in terms of employment), Isobel is a hybrid expert: as scientist and business entrepreneur. Asked about GM food risk, she responds as follows.

As I am microbiologist, I know exactly the kind of experiments, and I know about how they have been interpreted. There are risks, but it is not on the scale of what people are talking about for the most of things. I don't think it justifies the hysteria. But having said that, I do think the companies have a responsibility, especially if you are producing something that is going to go into consumer goods. You have to have totally different attitudes to producing something for that than if it is going to be for pharmaceuticals. I think Monsanto and other companies like them didn't realize that people will accept a vast amount of risk when it is a pharmaceutical and they will not accept the same amount of a risk for food [even though] the process is the same and the health and safety issues the same. They horribly miscalculated because they are basically scientists, most of them, and they knew the risk was the same.

Interestingly, this is Isobel as business-entrepreneur (knowledgeable about the 'customer') telling us that 'basically scientists' don't know their 'clients' like good business-people do. We recall that earlier, in criticizing the banks, she said that business was not like science with 'just one or two ways of doing things', and she now illustrates this scientific 'binary' mind-set in relation to the BSE crisis:

I used to work in a hospital and all the scientists I knew had one or two attitudes towards BSE. There were those who had totally given up eating all beef from the very, very first announcement and there were quite a lot of those. And the other ones just laughed and would eat beef, the kind who actually went out to the supermarkets when the beef crisis first happened and bought up sides of cows and put them in the freezer. They were absolutely [saying], 'Well, there is a risk, it is very small'. Those are the only two attitudes.

Yet, Isobel *also* still self-identifies as a scientist, as in the following account of GM science:

That particular experiment with that potato toxin given to rats – I think if you genetically modified potatoes or plants to produce something toxic you shouldn't be surprised if animals get sick when they take it. So, I think it was a bad experiment. But, it was very enlightening to see the response from the public. I think it proved that the scientific education of most people in this country is just so bad *and* also that the companies are not getting their message across properly. But on the other hand, yes, there is risk, of course there is. You don't know all the possibilities of genetic outcomes of modification, you don't, there's no doubt about it.

In the case of environmental science, where there are only 'one or two ways to do something', it is not the banks (or government) who are at fault, but an ignorant, unscientific public (whipped up by a media that 'sensationalizes pretty much everything'). And yet Isobel sees that scientists, too, are part of this public; and she herself gives a clear example of how, in response to the

BSE crisis, scientists' responses and choices are *cultural* and about *consumption* (rather than explicating the 'babble of voices' within science *as profession* which Beck focuses on). As 'basically scientist', Isobel admits to the 'incalculability' of this science: 'yes, there is a risk, of course there is.' But in her view, as business entrepreneur, 'An amount of risk is healthy. You can't live without any risk, it makes life boring.'

Isobel brings together a range of 'professional' expertises: her business knowledge (based on the acquisition of an MBA), her science as a molecular biologist, and her personal risk competencies (though she feels she needs to do more training to control better the risks of 'extreme' skiing). Unlike Ian and Keith's cases, big companies do not dominate her sense of risk. Nor do the media, even though she undoubtedly thinks the media have power. Rather, Isobel can pick and choose according to her situational circumstances which aspects of the media might help her (or her family) with various aspects of risk. For example (in this case like Ian) she has encouraged her young daughter to watch *Coronation Street* because of its 'classic' treatment of a 13-year-old girl who gets pregnant. 'So I did make a point of making her watch that episode, and said, "Look, see!"' In the case of GM food, her answer lies in a better science education in schools. But, for her, scientists, themselves, are not an adequate circuit of communication in risk matters. When it comes to Monsanto and the GM food crisis, Isobel suggests that it is the scientific mind-set itself which lies behind Monsanto's 'miscalculation'. Her GM food story is there to indicate that scientists tend to think in absolutist or binarized ways with 'nothing in between'. The suggestion is that reflexivity about their own contextualized responses to the BSE food crisis should have taught scientists how powerful a myth food is in our cultures (compared with pharmaceuticals).

Isobel, in fact, perceives what Beck calls the 'world risk society' as one of plural rationalities, and she discerns order and pattern in risk-taking behaviour provided you 'spend a long time thinking and be more creative'. In this important sense, Isobel's stories illustrate Beck's (1992: 16) point about competing rationalities in a new situation of growing competition between overlapping discourses of risk. In the area of economic and financial risk she describes a terrain of choice and constraint, articulated as a dialogic relationship between the creative risk-taking of the 'good' businesswoman and the controlling caution of the banks. As a businesswoman/scientist, she again articulates a dialogue of risk between the 'need for more research' on GM (as virtually every other high-tech interviewee insisted also) and the 'creative thinking' of entrepreneurialism.

A clear pattern among the high tech professionals we interviewed in Oxfordshire was this 'dialogic' subjectivity. They *needed* a range of media forms. Like most manufacturing workers, they were often suspicious of a 'sensationalist' mass media. But unlike them – unlike Ian reactively seeking the 'latest' on Rover from the local radio or firm Internet site – these high tech people scanned the Internet in advance (to research the GM food issue, or to check out that the places where they were holidaying abroad were safe, or to look up health information personally relevant to them). They looked for information in a surprisingly wide range of media sources, which often included literature produced by non-government organizations, Greenpeace subscriptions, even *Private Eye*. And a number had 'insider' information from other scientists in the pharmaceutical or agribusiness companies that are situated nearby in Oxfordshire.

'Invisibility' and 'incalculability' were consequently less of an issue both experientially and in terms of a variety of circuits of communication for these high tech people. In many cases, like Isobel they had a convenient risk 'world view', a confidence in their flexibility in new knowledges to match the flexibility of the economy (even when they worried about the crime tendencies or 'economic dependence' characteristics of those who did not), and frequently they gained as much pleasure in their 'no job for life' status as in their 'extreme' leisure pursuits, where they spoke confidently of their expert training courses in 'aggressive down-hill skiing', 'coastal navigation sailing', and so on. Certainly some worried, with Beck, about the environmental or biotechnological future; but their more consistent worry was with the 'increasing gap' between the 'computer-literate' and those who 'cannot adapt, cannot evolve'. This anxiety then fed into increasing fears of crime, especially for their children (significantly the only 'interest group' to which any of our Oxford high tech interviewees actively belonged was Neighbourhood Watch).

Henry

Henry, 49, is the company director of a high tech firm. According to his account, this university science-educated high-tech boss knows all about how capitalism works, and what the Thatcher government did to destroy the traditional industrial base. He immediately observes that although people are better off financially, social values are declining because of such factors as 'economic internationalization, globalization, capitalism, the media pushing selfish values'. According to Henry, risks are significant, and probably increasing. He identifies the following as the most serious risks facing Britons:

Environmental risk caused by the massive pollution in our society and by industry and all government bodies failing to act. I think [there are] risks from lack of security and safety by poor policing. Risk from financial disaster, the risk of losing your job, so it is quite a risky world. The environmental risks are from cars, chemicals and lack of a decent [regulatory body]. The risks have changed over my lifetime. Everything is more urgent, therefore there are greater risks caused by the urgency. Ten years ago there was significantly less chance of people who work for companies for a long period of time losing their jobs. Now it is unusual for people to work for companies for a long time. So there are enormous expectations for people to change their jobs a number of times. There are some people who have been unable to cope with that.

Despite being in a high tech workplace himself, Henry has a cynically realistic view of the enterprise, and how it came to be in the forefront of government policy. He thus describes the most important risk facing Britain as 'the destruction of our manufacturing base by a government solely encouraging high-tech businesses and allowing the financial world to create incredibly high values and companies that are probably not worth those valuations'.

Henry is a significant risk-taker financially and on the roads, commuting long distances on motorways to work. But it is different with health risks, and he is extremely cautious about GM food. He is concerned about the lack of hard information available to assess the risks, and likens it to the situation with nuclear energy:

> I think there is a serious risk with GM foods because I don't think the companies who play around with genetics have ever done enough to be sure of the implications. To take any major advance in science in this kind of way – like nuclear energy – people haven't researched that well enough.

Henry is critical of the government for failing to act as a watch-dog in this matter and not imposing safety standards on companies. He knows from experience in high tech companies the risks that they will take to make a profit or cut costs:

> I have worked with genetically modified organisms, and there are companies that are extremely disreputable companies who would play around with genetically modified organisms. At the end of the day they have to make some money, and probably with the exception of the big companies like Monsanto (who also play around with it), all these companies have little money, and when you have little money you cut corners and you take enormous risks. A lot of bio-tech companies have no money at all, and they are the ones who are doing a lot of the work on genetically modified organisms. So when you have no money you do things in a very low quality way.

All in all, this is a street-wise science-educated capitalist high-tech entrepreneur, who knows how to play an economic game he doesn't particularly like, and is, for specific British political-historical reasons, risky. But behind that company director dashing between his home and place of work by car, there is also a scientist viewing the world in a much less cavalier way. He has to be both, because one way or the other the global costs might otherwise be too high:

> Many years ago I worked in the fertiliser industry, and we said then that nitrates in the water were not a problem at all. Yet they are, and it is simple things like that that come back and hit us and cause the quality of life to be appalling for certain groups of people. Everybody wants to make money and you probably hope you have taken your money out and run away before whatever comes and happens to the share price. And that seems to be the way of life. There is no choice [but] to go globalization.

Henry is taking his high-tech money and running before the industry crashes, while also watching for the red lights of Beck's 'catastrophic' world risk society. He consumes risk in a personally reflexive way, playing off, and performing in our interview – a variety of identities: anti-capitalist, successful entrepreneurial capitalist, scientist – with the stated confidence to 'surf' each wave of risk threat and opportunity that comes along. Above all it is – as with our other high-tech Oxford interviewees – his confidence in his 'scientific literacy' which integrated his performance of self in the interview situation.

Concluding comments

We noted in our Introduction that 'invisibility' (of environmental risk, and of the old, centralized workplace) and hybridity (of 'class/industrial' and 'risk' modernity) are two of Beck's most foundational themes. He has been criticized for his reliance on 'meta' concepts which elide issues of power, as well as conventional 'modernist' categories like gender, class, age and ethnicity. However, we have questioned in this chapter the broader criticism of Beck: that his theory logically eschews empirical research. By drawing on the work of social geographers, we have indicated that this empirical work is both productively under way, and that some of it (with minor extrapolation indeed from Beck!) does blend analysis of (capitalist) power with 'glocal' and embodied research. Here the synthesis between 'macro' analysis of the continuing logic of profit-oriented rationalization (which Beck emphasizes in his sense of a hybrid modernity) and the fraught and uncertain micro-worlds of individualization and risk biography has been valuable.

We have seen in our Oxfordshire case studies, also, that *lay understandings* of this particular synthesis are common. Moreover, the Rover car workers we discussed clearly indicated their sense of a *causal* narrative of risk (in which Beck's 'disenchanted' family is central). Here, the (hidden but experientially understood) forces of multi-national capital were seen to be establishing a dystopic future which binds together a wide range of risk subjectivities, including education, health, family separation and fear of crime. In these risk biographies, the narrating ego was indeed a methodological device at the centre of 'family and wage labour, education and employment, administration and the transport system, consumption, pedagogy, and so on' (Beck, 1992: 136). However, our own methodological device of in-depth interviewing revealed that continuing 'wage labour' – 'a job for life' – was the narrative 'initial situation' in many of these risk biographies.

In the case of our high-tech interviewees, 'a job for life' was a constant discursive *object* (when speaking about other people's risk concerns, emotional breakdown, even resort to crime). But Beck's 'risky underemployment' was consistently mobilized by these interviewees as a positive aspect of multiple risk identities (financial, health, fear of crime, extreme sports and so on) which engaged with more 'traditional' structures on the pathway to 'improving the situation'. Thus banks were criticized for being too cautious about risk, and both minor and major pharmaceutical companies were also frequently criticized, both for 'cutting corners' on behalf of profit, and for the lack of *cultural* flexibility and sensitivity, which high-tech interviewees believed they had in abundance.

This is not to say that the high-tech interviewees did not *also* describe a dystopic British future. 'New economy' and 'class/industrial' interviewees alike often had a clear sense of the relationship between power, 'macro' corporate (and governmental) strategies, and the fears, uncertainties and anxieties of 'individualization'. But the difference was that high-tech interviewees tended to generate *two* narratives, one (personally optimistic) about 'surfing' these economic uncertainties; the other a dystopia (among those educationally and emotionally unqualified) of poverty, crime, and family breakdown. Our 'new economy' interviewees described this 'other' world regularly and relentlessly. As one would expect, members of this latter group varied in the degree to which they felt that their own (and Britain's) scientific/technological competence would 'risk manage' this 'other' dystopia. But almost without exception, our high-tech interviewees also spoke about this potentially dystopic future, and many worried for their children.

Most interviewees (as Beck would predict) felt the 'immiseration' of risk-distribution. But the 'new economy' people felt it indirectly; and sought to ward it off via a wide range of discursive (e.g. specialist media and 'insider') sources of information. They were able to draw on not just a broader range of news media, but critical-satirical magazines (*Private Eye*), environmental interest group literature (Greenpeace, Friends of the Earth), the Internet (for a wide range of leisure, health and environmental risk issues), direct personal experience of the media as expert informants, as scientists actually working for multinational companies, as well as previous experience as scientists both within academia and other (earlier) 'risk' industries.

As Beck describes, these were the citizens of risk modernity who were fully aware that science is a plural and uncertain set of systems, but for whom there was a 'depth of dependency on knowledge, which surrounds all dimensions of defining hazards' (Beck, 1992: 53). They were, thus, as Beck (1992: 52) says for his new risk citizens whose 'consciousness (knowledge) determines being', in the business of *actively informing themselves* via a discrete range of circuits of communication. These interviewees were all (women as well as men) 'rationalist', seeking 'fact' out of media 'opinion', and 'balancing' their sources of risk information in order to 'make my own decision'. They were, therefore, all confident about their own ability to control most (but not all – e.g. environmental and crime) risks. They knew how to be 'risk reductive', feeling able to draw on their superior education and access to information to do so. But women as well as men frequently also sought 'affect' in the 'adrenalin buzz' and risk of extreme sports, and they were inclined to see parallels, even causalities, between their economic and leisure risk activities. Nevertheless, here too, control (via training in expertise) was regarded as essential to pleasure.

It may not be the case that the majority of these people are active in what Beck calls the new sub-politics, but they are certainly aware of its importance.

They may still be in 'collusion' with Beck's 'techno-economic system', but they work with it via multiple identities, and in some cases are even able to be reflexive about their performativity in 'surfing a wave' which they deeply distrust. Even those few who believe in a natural evolution where 'science = progress' seem haunted by that 'other' (but contiguous) world of a 'transient', 'fragmented' or 'dependent' culture, which has infiltrated even their small Oxfordshire villages.

Car workers like Ian, on the other hand, continue to reside in a labour market in which, to quote Beck:

> the determinants of the class situation – the loss of a job, for instance – is evident to everyone affected. No special cognitive means are required for this, no measuring procedures, no statistical survey, no reflections on validity, and no consideration of tolerance thresholds. The affliction is clear and in that sense *in*dependent of knowledge. (1992: 53, original emphasis)

Nor, as we have seen, does Ian have the information sources (beyond the local radio news breaking on the hour, and his desperate and reactive resort to the company's own website) to give him any more sense of certainty and control. Ian is *in* the other interviewees' narrativized dystopia. They describe the same set of risks (going well beyond Beck's obsession with environmental risk) as the high-tech interviewees. Risk modernity is not – *pace* Beck – 'universal and unspecific'. It is specifically (i.e. economically and locally) situated, and historically and globally contextualized, by individuals in both the 'new economy' and 'class modernity' sectors.

The hybridity of these different economic systems is never clearer than when both groups speak about their common fear of crime, and yet speak about these fears via different (monological or dialogical) discourses. For Keith, losing his 'job for life' will generate a unilinear narrative, threatening family separation, loss of schooling and health facilities, financial impoverishment and greater fear of crime. For the high-tech interviewees, no element of this dystopic story is different. But their tales are post-modern, multi-identified, 'individualized', and confident. They are, as one of these people put it, of the new 'warrior class' empathizing with, but distant from, the 'dependent' Britain of the 'victim class'. Beck is right that risks are perceived as interwoven into the life course, and interconnected rather than separated across different boundaries. But the tellers of these risk biographies are differently situated as the subjects and objects of their tales, however much they are (equally) aware of the sources and expenditures of power.

We have been arguing here that Beck's overall thesis is far more productive in thinking about risk and the everyday than his critics often give him credit for. But his risk society thesis tends to focus too much on science's radical engagement, with science as a profession of 'counter-critique'. This is valuable, and important in any further research on risk performance and representation in different media genres. But (as Isobel's BSE story about scientists suggests), we need to be examining scientists as hybrid citizens and consumers in their everyday lives also. Moreover, that 'everyday' will include what Beck calls 'new forms for the division of labour within the relationship of science, scientific practice and the public sphere' which go beyond the *intra*-scientific 'babble of voices' he focuses on. They will also inhere (as in Isobel's case) in a voiced division of labour between 'reflexive scientific' and 'entrepreneurial' identities. In which case the 'overlap' between 'instrumentalist' and 'reflexive scientization' is likely to be far more persistent and complex than Beck's risk society thesis seems to imply.

5
Plural Rationalities: From Blitz to Contemporary Crime

[A] cultural perspective on risks unmasks a world of plural rationalities, it discerns order and pattern in risk-taking behaviour and the beliefs that underpin it. As Beck states, what is at stake in the risk conflicts of today is not so much risk avoidance, as the definition of risk in this new situation of growing competition between overlapping discourses of risk. (Lidskog, 2000: 216)

Our Oxford interviewee Isobel's stories about risk (discussed in Chapter 4) illustrate Lidskog's point. In the area of economic and financial risk she described a terrain of choice and constraint, articulated as a dialogic relationship between the creative risk-taking of the 'good' businesswoman and the controlling caution of the banks. Leisure-time risk-taking was perceived as a functional outcome of this, as many businesspeople in Isobel's network turned to 'extreme sports' to mobilize the risk-taking she saw as fundamental to the human spirit – this latter ideology of human enlightenment thus working as a master narrative of 'order and pattern in risk-taking behaviour'.

As a scientist herself, Isobel was much more cautious about describing 'overlapping discourses of risk'. And yet even here, her story about other scientists' personal response to the BSE crisis (whether to eat beef or not) indicated that scientific rationality, as Lidskog says, is 'shaped by historical and social factors, meaning that expert judgment inevitably involves contextualized knowledge' (Lidskog, 2000: 212). And when it came to Monsanto and the GM food crisis, Isobel suggested that it is the scientific mind-set itself which lay behind Monsanto's 'miscalculation'. Her GM food discourse was there to indicate that scientists tend to think in absolutist or binarized ways with 'nothing in between'. The suggestion was that reflexivity about their own contextualized responses to the BSE food crisis should have taught scientists (and Monsanto) how powerful a *myth* food is in our cultures (compared with pharmaceuticals).

Klaus Eder has argued that the real 'risk' in the risk society is not technological outcomes as such, but increasing social differentiation – hence the many pluralities of subjectivity and knowledge which Lidskog finds in both scientific and social knowledges. The replacement of corporatist and command economies by 'horizontal systems of negotiation among collective actors' (Eder, 2000: 229), has meant increasing complexity and differentiation of values and goals. Although Eder is over-functionalist in his risk theory (at the expense of issues of power that we looked at in the previous chapter), his point is helpful in balancing Beck's over-emphasis on environmental risk.

For Beck, the invisibility (and spatio-temporal uncertainty) of global environmental risks produces a high degree of public risk anxiety, which experts with competing views do little to assuage. But our Oxford interviewees, Isobel and Ian, were not especially anxious about genetic technology and the environment. Isobel thought there had been (media-induced) public 'hysteria' (as most interviewees with a scientific and/or high-tech background have also tended to say to us). Ian simply got on with the job of eating his genetically-modified canteen Cornish pastie and trusted in regulators and experts. However, in what was for both of them a central area of risk preoccupation and anxiety – economic risk taking – they both complained of what Eder calls 'corporatist' and Lidskog calls 'synoptic' policy-making and planning.

Lidskog describes synoptic planning as 'a one-way process of communication exchange. Its purpose is to inform the lay public, not to see ordinary people as providers of useful knowledge or as legitimate actors who have the right to influence the planning process' (2000: 204). Isobel's banks ('safety-Nazis') are synoptic planners; and so too is Ian's BMW corporation (and the government that chose BMW rather than Honda to take over at Rover without consulting the employees).

Both Ian and Isobel would undoubtedly favour, in their economic affairs, Lidskog's alternative to synoptic planning: *dialogical incrementalism*, where 'planning experts are only one among many voices' (Lidskog, 2000: 205; see also Boholm and Lofstedt, 1999). Lidskog's dialogical incrementalism is close to Eder's institutionalized discourse, which 'presupposes horizontal systems of negotiation. While in the vertical case you need to command, in the latter case you have to talk – often endlessly. Discourse becomes functional precisely when strategic action leads to bottlenecks – assuming no one wants the system to fail' (Eder, 2000: 229). Reflexivity (as in Beck) becomes central in the society that '*stages discourse*', where '[g]oals are no longer seen as part of an established value system or an ontological order; rather they become part of a social process within which goals are defined and redefined' (Eder, 2000: 229).

Eder's contrasting of dialogic negotiation to corporatist (top-down, expert-driven) 'strategic action' should not be taken to indicate that this is a 'resistance' paradigm of communication meaning (as, for example, in de Certeau's much used opposition of strategy to tactics). It is not the tactics of the poacher that risk theorists like Eder and Lidskog are looking for, to counter the instrumental rationalism of experts' synoptic thinking. Lidskog is quite clear about this, asserting that lay knowledge should not be privileged over scientific knowledge, for '[t]o replace an uncritical trust in one form of knowledge with uncritical trust in another kind means that the dichotomy between lay and expert is still in operation' (2000: 217). As an alternative approach he suggests transcending 'the tension between synoptic planning and dialogical incrementalism, between the knowledge of the expert and the knowledge of lay people' (2000: 217). The point is to incorporate both expertise and the 'situated' context in a new communicative practice that 'can encourage all relevant perspectives to contribute to environmental decision-making under conditions of profound uncertainty' (Cohen, 2000: 25).

If we are to go far with Eder's point that the environmental focus of risk debate is the symbol rather than the substance of the risk society, then it is not just environmental decision-making. Ian and Isobel – like many other interviewees in the UK and Australia – certainly indicate the usefulness of Eder's view that the 'risk society' be defined as one that 'stages' or performs discourse:

> Because decisions in modern societies are always risky – as indicated by contradictory, expert-based evidence and by uncertainty regarding the consequences of decision – the only way out is not to produce 'correct' answers but to generate decisions for which everybody takes responsibility. (Eder, 2000: 244)

In a central sense, our book, with its research focus on case studies and voices of 'lay knowledge', is a deliberate move to avoid 'correct answers' on risk. Obviously, the interweaving of our own discourses with those of our interviewees in these pages is a deliberate 'social mechanism' to 'facilitate the interaction and complementarity' of 'lay' and 'expert' knowledge (Lidskog, 2000: 25). In addition, though, there has been our emphasis on the empirical and the 'glocal'. 'Dialogical discourse' is situated discourse, 'staged' in time and place; and in this chapter we examine the interview performance of 'plural rationalities' in Coventry.

Coventry: 'the Blitz' as plural discourse

In Coventry, the Blitz of World War II is still a live memory for some, and a living myth for many others. The courage, the community, the steadfastness and resilience of Coventry people then becomes, in talk, a touchstone of 'the past'. World views of the present – good or bad – are often built upon it.

> I think years ago everyone was a lot happier with their lot whereas today ... I think people's expectations are just so high. I don't know where it comes from but it is the same with children now. By the time they are old enough to have things they have had everything and they are bored mindless, whereas when I was younger we had things that suited our age. I suppose I think about the war times. Not that I was alive in the war, but certainly what you see and hear, people were a lot more helpful towards each other. Like now, with petrol [shortages] everyone goes beserk over a loaf of bread, whatever. If it's a Bank Holiday [and the shops are shut] people go mad, and I think, God, what about in the war when you couldn't get anything? People survived and were a lot happier doing it. I think mentalities today are different. (Sandra, 56-year-old University administrative assistant)

I think people's attitudes have changed a lot towards risk, people will assume that other people should protect them more nowadays than they used to. Thirty years ago, I am guessing that people protected themselves and considered their own responsibility, apart from things they couldn't handle. It might be the Blitz, the risk of being bombed in the war – that was pretty risky compared to the risk of terrorism today. You were in so much more danger during the war than you are now, and yet probably the reaction to it was not as panicky then as it is now. (Jason, 31-year-old IT Manager)

The Blitz came up as a running theme in Coventry, in a way it did not in the other British cities. But, of course, it was not the only discourse of 'Coventry' that circulated among our 'risk' interviewees. Indeed, as the excerpts above indicate, 'the Blitz' was inflected in terms of quite different histories of Coventry. For Sandra, Coventry's Blitz was a benchmark time for a lost and regretted moral order, where people thought about each other, not materialistic possessions. In this case, the Blitz became simply a local inflection of a deep malaise we found in all three British cities which related to a sense of loss of community, increasing crime and violence, and a serious concern for one's children and grandchildren. In the case of Jason, the Blitz introduced another kind of world view – also found among our Oxford and Cardiff interviewees – which invoked risk as the motor force of a satisfactory personal 'success' biography, and at the same time often complained about other people wanting 'everything to be done for them'.

So Coventry-at-war was invoked as a benchmark against which two different narratives of decline were measured. These two narratives could, of course, overlap in so far as, in Lidskog's world of plural rationalities, it is quite possible to invoke a celebratory narrative about risk around one's personal identity and a narrative of decline for society generally.

But in all these cases, the Coventry 'Blitz' story is made to work in the context of other Coventry histories:

- Coventry's proud motor industry past (which despite its decline still supports 8,500 jobs in the city, and with car-related employment at seven times the national average);
- Coventry's rapidly diversifying economy (so that the service sector now accounts for 72 per cent of jobs, with the County Council as the largest employer), including considerable growth in communications technology, IT and the clothing sector;
- A very considerable overseas immigration into the city, with ethnic minority residents making up 12 per cent of the population, twice the national average (the clothing industry, which is a low skill, labour intensive industry dating back in Coventry to the 1970s is primarily an Asian family-run small business sector).

Inevitably, these different Coventry histories have also deeply determined the city's social geography. Jason, the IT manager, lives in Earlsdon, an increasingly embourgeoizing former working-class terraced area, whereas another of our interviewees who talks about the Blitz, Mike, 62, is a retiree who worked as a senior manager in the car industry and lives in a large country house some miles outside the city. Often these relationships between history and geography are reflected upon in our interviewees' narratives of risk.

All three of the Coventry interviewees we have mentioned above fear the current rate of crime. Sandra locks her car doors whenever driving alone. Jason talked about his recent experiences as a victim of theft, and how aware that had made him of the risk of crime. For Mike, while life in Britain appears better economically ...

socially, it is significantly worse because of the behaviour of people, because of violence, because of drugs, because of people's inability to bring their children up to understand what is socially right and wrong. I'm very fearful of the way things are going socially. I see it as disintegration in society. I would no sooner go down into Coventry late at night than fly in the air.

It was things flying at night in the air – German bombers during the Blitz – that represent Mike's earliest fears of risk. Now it is the 'peacetime' streets of Coventry at night that seems to frighten most of our interviewees, male and female alike.

Yet this is still too simplistic a tale of risk. Coventry's 'night' historics are not woven via simple binaries of past wartime and present violence in this way. It is true that 'Coventry' for a number of our interviewees signifies the resilience and comradeship of wartime, and that this provides a mythical template for troubles of the present. One older woman, for example, draws on the 'tough times in war' analogy to gloss the new economic diversification in the city.

There is lots of technology and lots of commercials – there is hardly any car manufacture here now. I think it shows that Coventry is made of tough stuff and they pick themselves up off the floor and that they put all their eggs in one basket in the beginning, which I suspect they won't do again.

It is also true that fear of crime ranks high as current 'risk' for nearly all of our interviewees.

But those two moments of violence – the Blitz and the current crime wave – are not book-ends to their stories. Coventry's 'institutionalized discourses' of risk have their origins in other places and other times: in immigration and ethnicity; in age and the gendered body; in myths of capitalism and the enlightenment project; in life-histories experiencing class mobility within both old and new sectors of the economy. *Pace* Beck and Eder, institutions such as class, state, religion, and science still play a major part in constructing our 'plural rationalities'. The more detailed risk biographies of Jason, Mike, Sandra and other Coventry interviewees will help illustrate this as we put to them – in our 'dialogically incrementalist' encounter – our own tales and categories of risk.

Capitalism, generation and progress: Jason, Will, Steve and Catherine

Jason, the 31-year-old IT manager, believes in 'good capitalism', and that people need to take much more responsibility themselves for the risks they face. He says that life is getting better, both generally in Britain and for himself. Having been out of work after graduating, he is now financially very well positioned so that his main risk at the moment is whether to buy a house in London or not, in case the market crashes.

Jason recognizes that individually people's jobs are more at risk than they used to be, because job turnover is every three or so years in his business, and no longer for life. But he is completely confident in the marketability of his skills, and (as a single man) is quite prepared to move. More generally, he recognizes how capitalism works: but that's life!

> Big business will always try and cut corners to get the end result and unwittingly they will probably cause lots of problems like BSE. Corners are cut on cattle feed, everyone is dying of brain spongeilitis or whatever it is called. Whether or not they actually cause it, whether or not they are forced into it by the fact that they are in a competitive situation and they have to do better than somebody else, that is not their fault either, that is the way capitalism works. You have to do something cheaper than somebody else does or you will go broke.

In contrast, Jason recognizes that it is his own choice that he goes on smoking, or risks skin cancer from holidays in Spain, or doesn't take out critical illness insurance cover even though experts in the insurance business advise him to do so. But he takes, he says, a cost benefit approach to risk ('Risk means the amount you are willing to gamble – the amount you are willing to lose in order to get a benefit') as well as a statistical one.

An example of his 'cost benefit' approach to risk is that he has given up driving and taken to the bicycle, even though that makes him more individually vulnerable. But he notes that:

> If you had a car accident every two years then in a period of twenty years, you are going to have ten accidents and the chances of one of those being serious are probably quite high. So, if you think about it like that, that is quite a big risk. I would rather opt out of that one myself.

Jason is prepared to drill into his computer equipment even though he should call in a professional to do it, and realizes his firm is deliberately turning a blind eye to it. He is willing to risk eye problems from computer screens (again the company turning a blind eye) because he is paid well. He recognizes the relativity of perceptions of risk (noting that he would not have worried as much about property crime ten years ago as he does now because he owned far less). He also understands that poverty helps cause the crime he fears, but argues that not all poor people are criminals. Fundamentally, he believes, it is the parents who are responsible.

Overall, Jason argues, in the 'real world' risks happen and you have to accept that:

I worked in a building where they discovered asbestos on one of the floors. It could easily have been a building which had bad asbestos in it, the grainy stuff that gets into the air, and there would be nothing you could do about that. But, that is not a risk that *you* took, that is a risk of just working in the real world.

Jason sees the tendency of people to blame others for risk as a recent trend, and this is where he draws on his wartime Blitz example:

My assessment of it is that the risks are probably a lot less now than they were, say, 30 years ago. Years ago, I get the opinion, that people accepted the risks as part of everyday life and just dealt with them, whereas these days some of the time people would look at a risk and say, 'The government should protect me of that. My company should protect me of that', when in reality, 30 years ago it was just common sense just to protect yourself against that.

Despite his fear of crime, in Jason's perception, society is improving, and risks are in fact diminishing because of greater knowledge and sophistication:

I think more of the risks in the past were natural weren't they? Your health was at risk all the time because there wasn't an NHS, or there was an NHS but it wasn't as good as it is today or it wasn't as advanced. I think on the whole risks have been lessened over the last 30 years just because things have become more sophisticated. Everyone is much more aware of the risks and the simple risks have been taken care of. You know, with the health and safety standards and the heart shapes you get on products to say that this product is certified as safe by the British Standards. That has taken out a lot of the stupid risks out of life. But our perception of risk is once the older big risks have gone the smaller risks take on the same size as the old ones.

For Jason, the media need to be seen as part of this sophisticated system, notifying people about risk: although they are not always to be trusted. John's parameters of trust tend to be pragmatic. In terms of the public finding out about new risks …

I wouldn't trust the government that much; but at the end of the day, once something has been clear and cut and dried as a proper risk I think I would trust them to then come forward and to say it is a risk. I wouldn't trust big business at all frankly. It is in their interest to cover it up. The tobacco industry have been trying to cover up cancer things for at least 20 years. The media I would trust for a small while. I think they will take something that is a small risk and blow it up into a large risk but at least with the media you know if they start shouting about something then there is something there and then it is up to you to find out what sort of level of risk it is … So at the end of the day [to find out about risk] I think I probably will go best with friends and family and then the media.

Jason believes the media are responsible for 'disproportionate coverage' of the GM food issue, even though he does see a problem there in the long term:

I don't see a problem with it short term. I probably won't have a problem eating it. I think the long term it could have effects that they won't be able to predict. I don't think those effects are going to be huge, probably not anyway. But I bet you they don't know what they are either, and that is where I think the risk comes in.

On the whole, Jason sides with people who say we shouldn't grow GM food, and worries at what experiments might already have been done. But he is also a pragmatic capitalist. Though he blames privatization in part for the

Paddington rail crash (because 'when there are 20 companies responsible, no one need take responsibility'), he nevertheless thinks the media have blown it out of all proportion, and believes, on capitalist risk-calculation lines ('Is one life worth the investment of a billion pounds?'), that probably the only possible solution was reached, given that there was not much rail investment earlier. When asked if he wants to summarize his thoughts about risk, Jason repeats: 'I think people consider themselves to be put at risk by other people when in fact you put yourself at risk. Nobody else does it for you most of the time.'

Will, 25, is a patent attorney, living in Earlsdon. This young 'knowledge' professional sees his move from secure employment to working in the private sector as his most risky undertaking – particularly when it comes to having to pass exams to stay employed. But it is one of the many features of 'capitalist society' that he is comfortable with. He recognizes that people without knowledge skills are more at risk (as society has shifted its needs from the 'physically strong' to the educated), especially if there is no safety net.

As regards his own position, Will is confident in his skills: 'in the sector that I work in I think there is a shortage of people to do jobs so if you are prepared to move around the country you will find another job elsewhere.' He certainly sees this kind of life as preferable to the more physically risky farm work that he was brought up with as a boy. There is more emotional stress in his current work, but he tries to cater for the risks of sedentary life by going to the gym. Like Isobel and her friends, he also sometimes deliberately takes physical risks like abseiling and driving fast to compensate for his sedentary work-life.

As an expert himself, Will sees the point in going to other experts, like financial advisers and gym trainers. But he is less convinced by the media, preferring to rely on his friends in the bio-tech industry than the media on the GM food issue. Like many other people that we interviewed working in or close to high tech, his main response here is 'more research'. Meanwhile, even though he recognizes that his friends could be too near to the issue to be objective ...

> I would rather believe them than the media because the trouble with journalists in this particular area is that none of them really know enough about the subject to write about it authoritatively. They go into writing about it with about as much knowledge as I do and it's probably less.

Will concedes that on many issues of major risk he has to draw on the media, but in most cases prefers to rely on his own experience or in colleagues he has learnt to trust.

Overall, Will has an 'enlightenment' view of the world. Knowledge is improving things, and risks today are an improvement on risks in the past when ...

> most of the health risks were due to either poverty or the fact that medicine, nutrition and sanitation weren't as advanced as they are now ... It wasn't really anybody's fault it was just the fact [that they weren't] as progressive as we are now.

This emphasis on medical and health improvement, so that 'all the old big dreads have disappeared' (including HIV/AIDS because of better education), is central also to the response of Steve (a 26-year-old motor dimensional control engineer), who believes that life is better for himself than his parents, and, while recognizing the past value of the welfare state, is not nostalgic for it. His biggest fear of risk is that the boom period of more money/more jobs he is experiencing will disappear. He blames the government for not reducing the price of the pound and thus protecting business exports, and the British standard of living falling further behind the European. He drives riskily in order to get to work on time.

Steve goes out on Saturday nights and so, he says, risks mugging, as does Lee (a 24-year-old insurance company customer service manager) who had been confronted by someone with an iron bar two weeks earlier, and Adam (a 23-year-old IT systems analyst) who says he was hit on the head by a man with an iron bar after he told him to stop shouting at a female friend. But though Adam thinks crime, mugging and rape are much on the increase, and worries about his girlfriend in that context, and though he sometimes drinks too much on a Friday/Saturday night with mates (sometimes skinny dipping in freezing water 'after 20 pints'), he, like Lee, argues that people are responsible for their own risks. Life, says Adam, is too short to stop taking risks: e.g. driving, planes, eating GM food (even though it could be a problem – 'we won't know for years'), travelling by train after Paddington ('you don't feel at risk unless you have been in a crash yourself'). Like the other young men mentioned here, he thinks money is people's biggest risk, and like most of them, acknowledges an increasing gap between rich and poor. But for Lee the 'me, me, me society is obviously paying off', and while Adam thinks lottery money should be used for homeless rather than for 'elite rubbish' like opera and modern art, he also feels that migrants should not be brought in 'by the lorry load' (at tax-payers' expense) while the country has its own economic problems.

All of our interviewee responses in this section have so far been male and young; but the 'enlightened capitalism' approach is clearly not gendered. Catherine, a 25-year-old marketing manager with a high-tech firm, living in the fashionable Birmingham suburb of Solihull, re-presents the stories we have been hearing above in her own, coherent narrative.

In interview, Catherine speaks of risk as embedded in two contexts: economic and techno-social. Economic risks are primarily those of the market. 'Big business to be fair obviously has to live by the rules and the nature of the economy and that is where [economic risk] comes from.' This is a 'must have' age; and 'more is expected of us, more is expected of our children, with the STATS tests and various other things they have to carry out throughout school; but [it is] better that there are more opportunities for people to develop both themselves and their careers further.'

This young woman sees herself as very much part of her age, her 'generation' – indeed, ahead of it in her willingness to take financial risks. Risk, in her definition, is 'being that tone step over the accepted norm'; and her own

89

exploration of financial risk has begun very early, ignoring the management training schemes her friends were on to set up her own marketing consultancy when she was 21, and at the same time buying her own flat and beginning to play the property market. At the time of her interview, Catherine was in the process of giving in her notice with one of the strongest marketing companies in Britain to go for a smaller company in Birmingham which seemed to offer more personal opportunities. 'I go for that sort of risk because that is to better myself as in individual, my social life, my career, so that is a risk I am prepared to take because in the long term the future prospects are much better, so I am happy to do that.'

Catherine argues that techno-social risks are primarily to do with technology and the pace of change; which is to do with 'the way that the technology has moved forward.We're living in a much faster society than say my grandparents did, down to a couple of weeks ago my Nan was saying, "What is this 'www' thing?", and so technology has moved on so much.' But not only technology has 'moved on': this young professional woman is also aware of the rapid change in sexual mores between her grandmother's and mother's generations and her own:

> Grandmothers didn't work, it was very much that they were given their money by the husbands, and until the '60s people didn't really sleep with anybody until they got married. Until the mid-'60s people weren't really taking a risk, but then since then, more and more pressure has led to people taking risks, just really to have their own identity.

This change has led to new risks for Catherine's generation, particularly to do with sexuality and STDs (including HIV/AIDS). Whereas Catherine takes risks financially, she is extremely 'careful' in her sexual practice; and has never taken drugs or smoked. Sexually, she is keenly aware of the 'big risk facing people our sort of age at the moment.'

Catherine is also especially aware of risks to the person, and would be cautious about going into Birmingham alone in the evening. Solihull, where she lives, is different; and she can go out in the evenings there. Again, the 'socio-economic' impinges here:

> because again, no disrespect, it is socioeconomic. Some of the inner cities like Liverpool, Manchester and that, I guess people do take more risks there. You have got people thieving, purely for some people just to live. There is a lot more [risk], but that is down to their background, so whereas here, I am lucky being brought up in a nice area with a nice life that you don't have to take as many risks.

Still, she does not intend 'to live in cardboard or a padded cell'. You 'have got to live your life'; 'I wouldn't not go into Birmingham on Saturday just in case I got mugged or just in case I got separated from friends. I wouldn't go that far, but, you have got to have in the back of your mind that you have got to be careful.'

'People our generation' is a key refrain in Catherine's narrative; as in all of the interviewees in this section. Steve, for example, says he is not so young that he takes the 'invulnerable' risks that he used to when in his late teens (fast driving, getting into fights with large groups of lads). But he is not so old either that he 'gets pessimistic about GM food and so on'. For Catherine, this positive 'generational' discourse has its own natural evolution, since 'the next generation' will go still further into risk-taking. She says:

Part of it is the economy as we touched up on earlier and part of it is individual and society, almost the pressures we are putting on ourselves. Children are expected to do so much at such an early age, they are not really children anymore. But that's inbred in them, so to be fair, by the time the five-, six-year-olds of today are 20, 25, they are going to take a lot more risks to stay that step ahead really, than the step ahead we are ahead of our parents.

Women working for the state: Tina

Tina is the personal assistant to the Director of Social Services at the Coventry Council. At 46 and working for 'welfare', Tina offers a sense of generational difference from Jason and Will that goes well beyond her biological age. She feels that life in general is worse than it used to be, because the new generation is much more materialistic, and she deeply regrets the lost community of wartime Coventry:

Before the war it was make do and mend, and during the war they had to. It seemed like that after the war there was a great optimism that the war had finished and people wanted in the main to enjoy life and to try and buy what they could. I think it has been a slow progression really, and that progression has been a breakdown in society because people are becoming far more materialistic in that way ever since the war. I think slowly, each generation has been very keen gathering materialistic things to the point where we are gradually becoming more interested in materialism than we are in one another as people.

Nowadays, at work in Social Services, Tina is often confronted by depressed and aggressive people who want to get access to her boss. Though working in Local Government makes her aware of the impact of legislation on people's lives, she does not blame the government for declining welfare standards:

I don't blame the government. It seems like people have forgotten their values. That is wrong because [we see at] Social Services a lot of people who are really struggling to survive, and because they can't get what they want they get extremely frustrated. Being the Director's PA they want to see the top man and they get me, initially. I try and put myself in their shoes, I try and appreciate where they are coming from and appreciate how frustrated they are. So, in a sense although they can get angry with me, I can relate to that and I try and understand their perspective.

But although Tina finds she can empathize with her clients, still 'I have to make a judgement about the level of risk as to whether I go down to see them, whether I need a security man, that sort of thing.'

Tina now contrasts the short-term risks of her childhood (when she was bullied and took positive action to end that, at her mother's advice) with the much longer-term risk-taking of later life (like getting married). Age is also taking its toll, as a cataract problem threatens her with blindness, and it is this, rather than other interviewees' fear of crime, which keeps her out of Coventry city centre at night:

> At night my worry more is whether I will see to get there rather than who will mug me. I think if you don't work in the city centre and you read the press, you could build up a fear of it, whereas if you work there day-to-day [like I do] and you know your way around, you accept it.

Still, Tina is one of the many female interviewees who always locks her doors when driving; and she is not altogether happy with 'asylum seekers', who she sees as the 'big current problem'. As a woman with 'welfare state' values, however, she puts a different spin on her talk here than some of the men we heard from earlier. Male asylum seekers, she argues, can be very arrogant, bringing their patriarchal values from their homelands to Britain (sometimes sweeping Tina and her mother off the pavement), and thus 'causing trouble with British people'. Tina's 'feminist' line here (and elsewhere), emphasizes that though historically risks for women have diminished (with the reduction of childbirth deaths and, later, the NHS), much still has to be improved.

Unlike the interviewees of the last section, Tina sees collusion between government and big business in both the GM food and the Paddington rail crash issues:

> I think my opinions were formed at that moment of the BSE issue. It is my cynicism maybe, but now when the government tells me that something is safe, I think well I need this in black and white from 20 scientists before I believe it, really. Unfortunately the link between government and big business is the key to government, and so they will not be separate from big business. They rely on them so they have to tread very carefully. And it is very easy to say 'Sorry' rather than 'No, we won't do it in the first place'.

Again, with the Paddington rail crash, Tina argues that:

> It is that link, isn't it, of the government and business – and whether, since it has been privatized, they are taking the necessary health and safety risks, or whether they are looking at their stock-holders and their profit margin. That is always there in my doubts. A question I always ask myself when I see one of these disasters is, 'Had it not been privatized, had the government still managed it, would that have happened?'.

Automotive dynasties: Marie and Mike

Marie and Mike, daughter and father, come from one of Coventry's automotive dynasties, in the sense that four generations of the family have progressively worked up from low-level jobs in the industry to middle or top management.

Mike worked up from being a technical apprentice in the auto industry to becoming Director of Vehicle Operations for the Rover Group, through 'being in the right place at the right time', as he put it. He says that he has 'always been a profoundly loyal company person, which is something I believe in absolutely fervently'.

Risk is endemic in the car industry, but Mike argues that he has always made a point of telling the Chief Executive if a long-planned and heavily invested product was not going to sell, because it is better to fail early than late. In any case, the auto industry is much better at programme managing and planning now than when he began in 1954, when 'the trade unions were very powerful'. So Britain is better economically than it was, but much worse socially, with violence, drugs, and youth criminality. Mike blames 'the television age' for this:

> When people first started watching television it was like the family units disintegrated. They used to send the kids out, 'Go away, don't bother me because I want to watch this box here. You can go and bother who you like'. That generation grew up and because they have never been taught any social manners or the way to behave or the way to be in control, they themselves have children [who] are coming from an even worse background.

Still, even in this one area of risk (of crime) which he fears, Mike does his best to take control:

> If you take the violence risks or the likelihood of being mugged, clearly you have some control over that by nature of two actions. One is that you avoid places where you know it's going to be prevalent, and the other thing which I practice now – since I walk a tremendous amount in my retired state because it is good for me – is you have got to be alert all the time and be aware of what is going on around you and be ready to take evasive action.

Risk, for Mike, is 'considered judgement', and he believes one is involved in this every day: walking, driving, working, getting in tradespeople who might rip you off and so on.

Although governments are sometimes implicated in creating risks (taxation, strength of the pound, etc.), the main culprit for Mike is the individual. Risks have changed over the years. There is less overt health risk today (e.g. the diphtheria, polio and other infectious diseases which Mike risked as a child). But, apart from social violence, things are better. He doesn't feel qualified to comment on GM food (he says that this is 'venturing into the unknown', and more testing is needed); and he is quite sanguine about the Paddington rail crash: 'The fact of the matter is that a train is driven by a human being and a human being is fallible.'

Still, this does not make Mike a fatalist about risk. Recently, he recounted ...

> My wife and I went on the train to Birmingham and we are sitting over one of the axles, and as the train accelerated and slowed down the axle on my side was making the most horrendous noise. I said, 'That, my dear, is a wheel bearing, without a shadow of a doubt'... I was so worried about it – and that's only the engineer coming out of me – that I walked up to the front of the train and told the driver and told him what carriage it was and said, 'There is something very, very serious with that. If you don't get it fixed soon that wheel is going to come off'. So what happened I don't know.

Mike doesn't in fact think that anything would have been done at all because of the economic factors concerned with taking a train out of service suddenly. But his anecdote gives a very clear example of Mike's philosophy that 'if you actually analyse it, the whole of life is risk management, it really is'.

Marie has graduated from being a secretary at Rover to management of stock control, with the encouragement of her boss who was Rover Group Systems Director. She ponders that nowadays her job would require qualifications that she didn't have, but she took her opportunity with both hands, worked seven days a week and through the night, and succeeded: 'Oh, I love it. I totally thrive on it, absolutely. I'm Rover through and through. I am a committed person, they can call me any time of the night, any time of the day and I'm just there.'

Marie's upwardly mobile work experience has made her *like* rather than fear risk, at least in the work context:

> I think I've been exposed to so many more risks as I've got older with the job that it has made me a stronger person and made me willing to take more risk. Whereas before I wasn't exposed to risk because I didn't really understand risk, and 'risk' is a frightening word so you try to avoid it. Whereas now risk isn't really a barrier for me.

Now, with her managerial salary, Marie no longer has to rely on her construction manager husband's income, and they can splash out on business-class holidays to 'risky' places like Mexico. Consequently, for her, 'risk' is a positive word: 'Risk *isn't* a "no-no" word. I go through risks everyday of my life with work. There is a risk with the system all the time, so we just plan around risk. Everything we put in, everything we do we always plan for the risks.'

Admittedly, other areas of risk are less appealing: trying to sell her flat in order to get the house they want (with the risk of losing the down-payment), walking alone at night to the pub (which she carefully avoids nowadays, always going with her husband or father); or marriage itself – moving from the security in both their cases of parents' homes directly into living together, and with very different personalities (she is loud, her husband quiet). Marie acknowledges that she has more control of risk at work than in selling her property, and she has had to work hard at overcoming the 'repel' factor in her early marriage.

Recently, though, Marie faced 'externally-induced' risks at work too:

> The risk I was exposed to when Rover and BMW split up, that was a risk not knowing if I was going to have a job or not. A lot of people looked for other jobs, but I thought they can't afford to get rid of the IT people just like that. Rover Group systems are all over the company, someone has to work on them, they have got to have people with knowledge. So I worked round that risk, I just carried on with that. I dealt with it carefully, though it was terrible coming home because I was worried sick really. You try to put a brave face on it, but it was very difficult.

Marie does believe that mistakes were made by BMW, in ignoring the local situation for too long and leaving too many of the old managers in place. She describes the terrible feelings there were when the news about BMW broke, without warning, and they were hounded by the media.

> It was awful and the *atmosphere* – I went down the track in car assembly 1 at Longbridge and actually saw men crying. It was such a shock, for ourselves it was, we were completely hounded by the press. Whenever you went into work, whenever you came out, they were trying to get in the gates, over the gates, it was a nightmare.

One might think that – as in the case of Ian at Cowley in Oxford (Chapter 4) – the 'nightmare' was less the media response, than the complete lack of company knowledge of what was about to happen. But Marie, as 'Rover through and through', is corporately loyal. She does blame 'authorities' for some things (but not for inflation, unemployment and so on). Though the GM food issue doesn't exercise her mind at all, she thinks hyperactive children could be at risk from GM, and blames government, companies and scientists a bit for that. Similarly she blames the government for learning nothing and doing nothing from the Paddington train crash (another UK train crash had happened the day before the interview).

The government is also at fault, she says, for not putting more police on the streets, and when you call them, they don't come. So she takes control over her own safety, locking her car doors when driving. And in her greatest area of risk – property purchase – she goes to advisors on mortgages.

Overall, Marie is satisfied with the way in which people's demands are higher today and so to some extent risks are higher. But as a result, '[p]eople are earning a lot more money than what they ever did years ago. So people have got bigger lifestyles, a more expensive way of living compared to what they were years ago'. She has taken plenty of risks at work and has made some mistakes. But she has, she says, always admitted these to her boss. She feels that being thrown in the deep end with her more responsible job has strengthened her and made her much more confident:

> It was high risk because I had nobody working with me, risk because I had never done it before and I didn't think I had the confidence to do it. I was just frightened, but I survived because once I got into it, into the nitty-gritty, I was fine. It made me a better person, made me stronger, made me more self-confident. I can deal with anything now when it comes to the system, when it comes to work. You learn from your mistakes really, because you put yourself at risk in the first place. You can listen to other people, that's fine but there is nothing better than your own experience. Overall, I've become stronger through risk.

Narratives of ethnicity and hybridity: Rajah and Farid

Rajah, 59, is one of the many Indian-born small business owners in Coventry's clothing industry. He has conducted a classic migrant story: hard work, family-oriented, educating his sons through university for better things. But so far the story has no happy ending, because 'everything is risk these days in this country'. His business is 'worse and worse', despite the hard work and risk-taking investment in new machines. His most recent major financial risk venture was in 1991/92 when he lost £120,000 in one day and could have gone into liquidation. But he took a further risk by taking out a mortgage on his property. Rajah's sons have completed their education now, but he is not convinced that they will get jobs. One is a lawyer and he blames 'jealousy' in the professions of law and medicine for limiting the number of jobs. Rajah has pensions, but does not know whether the companies he has invested in will go bust before the ten years he has to wait before he can benefit, and he fears losing all his money.

Rajah has tried to even out the business risk by co-operative ventures, but he feels that the experts he uses as consultants (working for the council) are too generalist and can't advise adequately in the clothing industry. He believes the government should do more to help small businesses, but instead you get MPs like his local one in Coventry who has himself gone bust in business, and Rajah suspects he is corrupt.

Rajah smokes, and worries about the risk involved with this practice. He is suspicious of GM food also. He suspects it is a risk but does not know whom to believe, distrusting the media. So, deprived of 'expert' knowledge, his take on GM food seems to follow a BSE model that 'something will come out, maybe five per cent or a couple of per cent. It won't be that bad but there will be something'. He sees big business like Railtrack profiting at the expense of public safety and was surprised and shocked by the Paddington crash. He also considers driving to be a risk because of more traffic on the roads and people not caring about others. He fears the risks of economic integration within Europe because of Britain's strong pound, high interest and high exchange rate. In our business, he says, 'We cut, cut, cut [the price]: we're just *keeping* the customer. We give them price what they want, but on the other hand the exchange rate is too high.'

Rajah's treasured family is also a problem. As he sees it, with sons nowadays there is always a risk when they marry, because they refuse arranged marriages and 'you don't know what sort of girl' they will marry. He has worked hard and taken risks for 17 years, but now 'we are back to where we started from'. Crime is worse, the environment is worse because of the 'cutting of costs everywhere. They are bringing in new ideas and systems and new things but I don't think they are getting any better.' And finally, he doesn't think the young generation will do for their children what his one did, making sacrifices and working hard for their future.

He does not see all of this as particularly a 'migrant risk' issue. He believes British people in general are facing risk in 'everything, everything'. It is more a generational than an ethnic issue, and he doesn't think he would do the same if he had his time again. 'Business – that is the worst part. If I knew the business was going to be like that, I wouldn't be in the business.'

Farid, 67, is a medically retired manual worker, who is married, lives in the tough suburb of Hillfields, and speaks Gujerati at home. In many ways he has a more optimistic approach to life and risk than does Rajah. Although this Muslim man was born in India, he is a long-term resident of the UK, and these two geographies dominate his two main perspectives on risk.

The first is economic. Compared with the poverty of his old homeland, and compared even with the poverty his community experienced in Coventry in the 1960s, 'life is a lot, lot better'.

People are far better equipped to lead a decent life than they were 20 or 30 years ago. In fact, to talk a little bit about my childhood, we were living in poverty and that was real poverty. People talk about poverty today, that isn't the poverty that we were in 30 to 40 years ago, here in Coventry in 1960, and that is poverty. Obviously, people a lot older than me will say that 1960 wasn't poverty, 1940 was, so it does go in cycles. But today with the benefit system – that is, the benefits that are attached to the housing, people have free medicines, free health care and everything else, to me, young people do not realize just how well off they are to, say, people like me 30 to 40 years ago. Then if we look at other cultures in Britain, I really should take some of these people that say they have got nothing to do, that they are bored, they haven't got a job, I could take them back home with me and show them what poverty is.

Farid's second risk perspective is cultural. Although he says he is not an 'extreme religious' man, he is a sufficiently devout Muslim to find buying food a risk:

Eating food, it certainly is a risk for me because I am a Muslim and being teetotal, although I eat meat I have to be careful, that the meat is hung out, which is a form of slaughter. So yes, buying something off the shelf in a supermarket, or even a halal shop, is certainly a risk for me. And then even having read the labels and all the long-term names that are attached to that food don't mean anything at all.

Farid also believes in an after-life, and it is from this perspective that he views new technologies as the greatest risk British people face:

Test tube babies, cloning, artificial foods, chemicals. With test tube babies, you will be able to order a baby off the shelf from Sainsburys! And that wasn't what it was meant to be. That isn't natural to me. Cloning, was it meant to be like that? Science has gone too far now. It's becoming very, very convenient, it won't be life anymore, it will be processed in stages – less human.

As with Rajah, Farid's cultural background also makes him a severe pessimist about his children's generation:

The government can do as much as it can, it can plough in millions or billions of pounds in to tackle crime and drugs, but at the end of the day it is society [that is responsible]. There is no discipline anymore, there is no respect for people, for the police or family. It is society gone mad, it really has and my actual fear is what kind of life that my grandchildren are going to be living. I have more fears because we haven't nipped this in the bud, but the more initiatives, the more schemes that seem to crop up, the worse the crime seems to get. It is society that has got to change.

On the one hand, then, Farid sees things in personal financial terms with some equanimity. As a much younger man he had, as he now acknowledges, taken a very big risk leaving what he saw as a dead-end job in engineering. He had underestimated his re-employability, yet, nonetheless, found himself not long later as a security manager with none of the 'factory slog, oil, dirt' he had been exposed to. And so he had been able to buy a derelict house on which he borrowed to renovate just in time for the property boom. Now, though retired on medical grounds, he still has a good pension. 'On that company pension, if I was to go back to my country of origin I could live very, very comfortably'. This would also help his acute health problems, which are made far worse by the damp British climate.

On the other hand, though, this kind of move would lead him directly into conflict with his own family-oriented cultural values, and the British cultural values of his children and grandchildren also, since they would not want to leave Britain:

It is a risk in terms that my three children would not want to go at all, and the standard of living in India is completely alien to this country. The languages, the traditions and everything else are completely different. I think I am prepared to take that risk and go back and live comfortably, with a view of doing some voluntary, charitable work there, with the money that I would have there.

Farid's understanding of GM food issues is stretched across this same sense of cultural hybridity. Thus his answer to a question about the risks of GM food is:

Yes and no. Yes in developed countries it might be a risk to people's health in the long term. Nobody is to know, it is early stages yet. But no, because there is so much poverty in Third World countries and that might be an avenue for people to get proper food.

Aging is also a major factor in his risk perception. Until his 30s he was a fit man, participating in a lot of sport. But since then his health has declined and much of his interview is a detailed description of his health problems and the care he tries to take with the food he eats. Probably for cultural reasons, and certainly for health reasons, he is a great believer in experts:

Certainly from the doctors, I do take advice. I try to follow that advice as much as possible in terms of eating foods, medication and even doing exercises which may sound silly but will help. It is those exercises which are actually [giving] all the pain, but there has got to be some sort of logic and I do follow that advice. Crime, again, you do have to listen to the professionals really because they should know what they are talking about. So yes, advice is important, people should listen and follow it as much as they can.

He carries this belief in experts to certain aspects of the media, believing in 'educational programmes' (like television documentaries) and broadsheets more than tabloid newspapers like *The Sun*, although he is aware of the political slant of all these papers. He is also aware in this area of the cultural divides that mark the relationship between his country of birth and his adopted country. He speaks of the class system he experienced at work in his younger days in England, with white and blue collar workers using different eating places, lavatories and so on. This, he believes, has now gone. But he still talks of the 'hell' the world is, where 'although we would all like to say that we all live together, still we are in divisions'.

Farid's view of divisions in society extends to his attitude to the Paddington rail crash, which appalled him because 'high enterprise came before personal safety'. Yet, as elsewhere in his interview, he also feels that 'we are all to blame'. Only three days later, when on a train he and others were complaining that they would miss an appointment because the train was going more slowly for safety reasons.

Overall, despite his feeling that life in Britain is getting better, Farid is not happy about it. He fears the increasing drugs and crime, and doesn't go out in the evening as he once did. He thinks that people are not being consulted enough about their futures, and that there should be more local initiatives involving people. His health is bad, as he is often in pain. He worries about his children and grandchildren. He is worried about new technologies and human values. Yet, his comparative references – both geographical and historical – make him aware that there are many positives too. And the media are better than they were:

> In terms of risks, you have got 24-hour news channels and a little bit more open about what they broadcast these days as well. The images [and] words are stronger so that does make you a little bit more aware of what is going wrong and how it is all going wrong and that probably does put a little bit of fear into you.

In Farid's case, age and ethnicity work together to make his perceptions of risk quite ambivalent; as symptoms of his own very practical hybridity.

Risks of the body: Gemma and Pat

Gemma is a 17-year-old female finance assistant with a housing trust who lives with her parents in Binley Woods. Among all our British interviewees, she is the one who spoke most about her sense of physical vulnerability. A protective boyfriend is very important to this young woman, who says that her mind 'works overtime' in relation to bodily risk.

It was an argument with a friend that led to Gemma walking home alone down a country lane at night a couple of years before. 'That was quite a big risk', she says, but she didn't think about it at the time: not until she read in the paper about another girl being raped there. She has a mobile phone, 'but nine times out of ten it's not charged up'. Instead she consistently has internal monologues with herself which sometimes lead her to take one action, sometimes another when out alone:

> When I used to go out with my friends we'd go into town and go out to a club and then they would all get a taxi, perhaps to somewhere else, and there would be me and a friend to get into a taxi. I wouldn't get into a taxi on my own, not at night. We would get a taxi back here but she would perhaps get dropped off. Sometimes I would say, 'I will get out here' and I would walk the rest of the way. Sometimes I would say, 'Drop me off at home'. Sometimes it is on how safe you feel.

Then, '[t]here is always the risk that if you put your drink down that it is going to get spiked. So perhaps you don't put your drinks down. Things like AIDS, you have to be careful of things like that and drug problems and that sort of thing, but I think it depends as well who your friends are.' Overall, Gemma feels extremely vulnerable 'because of my age and perhaps lack of experience, where someone older might feel safer'.

Soon, Gemma will be going on holiday to India, and sees herself as being faced with a panoply of risks there:

> There is a big risk there because there is a lot of disease over there, and there is the risk of the food as well because that is not cooked to the highest of health standards. You have to go to a doctor and get the immunizations because otherwise you would be risking your health in a very big style. Their roads and their standards of living in general are much lower and you take the risk that you are not going to get malaria or yellow fever or fall off the edge of a cliff because you hope that you will be able to control that. But things like illnesses, you can't always control that. You have the immunizations in the hope that it will.

Given her worries about food in India, Gemma's response to the GM food issue was interesting:

> I tend to be a bit blasé really, I ate beef when it was the BSE crisis. I like beef, you only live once that sort of thing. You have to trust the government to know what they are doing, and they don't always do the right thing, and presumably this is safe but it has been highlighted to be [risky]. You have to trust what people do because you haven't got an option and you don't know what you are eating really. We could have been eating it for years, but I think I would eat it and chance it.

Between a cautious trust in the ethics of government legislation and an alert media, she will take her chances:

> I would trust the government for now, but obviously they might bring out a story next week where they say it is completely unsafe. You have to keep an eye on what the media is telling you, but they don't always tell you the story as it is. You have to listen to what they are saying and just try and work out what they actually mean.

Gemma thus puts her muted trust in experts, though not quite in the same way that she relies on her boyfriend to protect her from direct physical risk. As she puts it, she by-and-large trusts the experts 'out there' because 'I've grown up with technology and I have seen it all really and it is changing so fast'. Further, she thinks that technology improves life rather than detracts from it:

> I would like to say that life is getting better because I think people are more aware of what is going on. The government are bringing in legislation to improve the quality of life and improve the way we live in general. The changes in technology [mean] that life is getting better. And I would hope that the government wouldn't bring in legislation that would make life worse, but we have to trust them really.

So media and government are half-trusted experts in informing her about these changes. Thus, 'I think you learn about risks from all sorts of areas, watching the news and just watching general television, reading the newspapers and speaking to your friends as well, because you hear things like, such and such has happened and don't go down there because that would be risky.' Television news, soap opera, the *Weekend Mail*, the local paper, all give her information, which she sieves through talking with friends. 'I wouldn't trust the media because they tend to exaggerate quite a bit on the stories just to get the readers, really. But I would trust my friends to tell me the correct story and they have no reason to tell lies.'

Gemma's is very much a story of local vigilance, reliance on her boyfriend, trust in her peer group, and cautious trust in experts and government in the global issues:

> I can't really think of any risks facing Britain as a whole. There are risks say from places like Birmingham where the economic situation of the town is at risk when they close the Rover plant. Risks where the government put areas at risk or other big businesses put areas at risk. I think the government and politicians put the country at risk sometimes, which wouldn't be in any of our control. When you talk about monetary issues, when they decide to do things with the pound or whatever it is that they do, they would be risking the country. Things like affecting the industries and exports. I think the government is responsible for a lot of the risks that society as a whole

takes, and people don't have the choice really of whether to take these risks, as the government don't always get it right.

Some things are getting better (technology, the health system – despite its long queues), some things are getting worse (personal crime). Gemma negotiates her path between them, drawing judiciously, often fearfully, on whatever resources she can.

Pat is a 67-year-old publican and retired/security manager, born in Ireland and now living in Hillfields, Coventry with his wife. He was formerly in the army, and this, he says, has shaped his view of risk considerably. He has seen active service in Borneo and Malaya (keeping the British interests safe against people trying to 'take over'), and was shot at in Cyprus as a UN soldier during the Greek/Turkish war. He had the job there of collecting dead bodies after killings, and learned to look after himself.

Army training gave Pat much of his later confidence in life: 'because I was training hand to hand. I think the army had a lot to do with the way I handled things.' This stood him in good stead as a publican later in life. He says he has physically cleared his pub of drug dealers, Hells Angels, men with knives and a variety of other miscreants (usually in close contact with the police). From him, his wife has also learnt how to handle dangerous customers.

Knowing how 'to handle things' is a leitmotif of Pat's interview. Though he is aware of unemployment, he believes that there are some people who can handle things and some who can't. He is one of the people who can: taking precautions (strong security measures to protect his wife after a burglary), looking around him after going to a bank, watching out in city alleyways. But though cautious, he is a man of action: and his narrative is full of incidents where he has controlled a difficult or dangerous situation, helped other people, sorted out young people (by talk as much as action), protected his wife, etc. He is very confident in his ability in this regard: 'I reduced the risk and made it harder for the opportunists'. He is medically very fit, hasn't seen a doctor for two years, and when he did was told he had the 'constitution of a bull'. In contrast to his story, he says there are the young people who 'can't see any future'. A couple of years in the army would soon put them right.

It was his army-based skills that led Pat into computer security; and he is now comfortably off (as is his wife). He contrasts this with the type of people who 'can't be bothered helping themselves', and points to the government's mistake in supporting 'scroungers and people who don't want to work'. As regards himself, 'I have got no worries, and no big things hanging over my head and no stress'.

Pat believes people are overwhelmed with the bad things they read in the paper. He is not overwhelmed, but rather made angry by seeing some people 'getting away with it'; and he worries about judges that give different sentences for the same crime because of 'mitigating' circumstances. Strong 'as a bull', Pat has no concerns whatsoever about GM food. He has read about it in the media as a risk, 'but I have not got into [it]'. Here is a big, confident, physically-trained man who has put his life together as a series of controls: from military security, through computer security, to pub security.

Concluding comments

As we suggested in Chapter 2, the set of questions that we asked about personal risk revealed some dominant perceptions, at Coventry as elsewhere:

- Embodied risks (physical and health risks, and the risk of violence: each of these with different age and gender constituents);
- Financial risks (linked to styles of 'new' and 'old' employment, supporting children and retirement, whether this latter was a comfortable, affluent retirement seen as a controlled continuity of one's work life, as in Mike's case, or enforced retirement, as in the case of Farid);
- Intimate risks (related to romantic, marital and familial relationships, as in Marie's 'repel factor');
- The risks of foreign travel (Gemma's worries about the perils of India) or migration (Farid's and Rajah's cultural ambivalence and hybridity about being a father of children in Britain);
- Work risks: the end of a 'job for life', and long-term redundancy.

Intimate and other risks could often work together as 'shared risk'. For example, one of the vulnerable Gemma's major worries is risking her relationship with her parents because of her boyfriend: 'You can risk the relationship of that by doing things that they would disapprove of.' Yet she relies on her boyfriend very heavily to protect her from bodily risk. This shared interviewee/parent/partner risk relationship is clearer still when linked to migration issues. As we saw in the case of Rajah, for example, many older Indian-born British parents disapprove of their children avoiding arranged marriages.

We also commented in Chapter 2 on the significant difference we found between the categorization of risk that individuals perceived as threatening people in their society and those they identified as threatening them personally. As we have seen, in Coventry, there was a major concern among nearly all interviewees about crime, coupled with a nostalgia (often with wartime 'Blitz' references) for earlier days when one's house doors could be left unlocked, in marked contrast to nearly all the women (and some men) in the Coventry group who nowadays lock even their car doors when driving. There was also some regularity in the blaming of government for not assisting enough with manufacturing or small business, because of taxation or monetary policies 'in Europe' (even Gemma, who tended to trust governments and didn't have much to say about risk beyond her own obsession with personal vulnerability, mentioned this in passing).

Yet, while governments tended to be blamed for economic matters, this was not often the main case in relation to crime. Here the 'individual responsibility' discourse (that we noted earlier as a dominant response to perceptions of personal risk) was readily drawn on to blame the individual perpetrator (or their parents) for the current level of crime, as in the case of Jason, Will, Mike, Farid and Pat. Often, this response was embedded in a 'new knowledge' high-tech evolutionist confidence in capitalism, as with Jason and Will, or in a 'working-class-made-good' managerialism related to life-time success in traditional high-wage industries, as in the case of Mike and Marie. Pat, like Mike, sees his life as one of long-term individualist continuity; in this case of his army-based physical 'strong-as-a-bull' confidence.

This is not to say that governments are not criticized at all by these rather varied successful men and women: either because it has not provided a 'safety net' for the inevitable 'walking wounded' in capitalism's necessary evolution (Jason, Will), or because it is being too soft on these people (Mike, Pat) – and there is an underlying current throughout the interviews of hostility to asylum seekers. But the dominant discourse in all these cases is one of individualized responses to social problems. Tina, who works for Coventry Council, has a sufficiently strong 'welfare state' ideology to both empathize with clients who sometimes threaten to assault her and to blame governments for making them like that. But this was the minority view, among all our Coventry group.

Despite these few examples, the individual's location in place and space – for these interviewees, 'Coventry' – was a strong positioning, while being inflected according to a layering and hierarchizing of 'personal' and 'social' perceptions of risk:

- Sandra's reference to people's talk of wartime Coventry in contrast to the new materialism;
- Tina's nostalgia for the community of wartime Coventry as a reflection of her disappointed welfarism;
- Jason's use of the Blitz as an example of a lost individualism;
- Mike's actual childhood memory of the Blitz now underpinning a confident life-narrative of 'considered judgement' in risk-taking;
- Pat's sense of nostalgia for another war-torn place, Northern Ireland in contrast – both Ireland now and Coventry now – to a newer world of over-lenient judges, pimps, prostitutes, drugs and crime; and
- Farid's knowledge of 'real' poverty in India inflecting his comparison of a much harder and poorer Coventry in the 1960s than now.

So while, as we said in Chapter 2, there was a difference in people's accounts in conceptualizing control when applying it to risks facing oneself as against one's country, this was not simply a binary opposition between 'individual responsibility' and 'government blame' discourses. Rather, these two risk discourses differed, blended or merged as 'plural risk rationalities' according to a number of other factors of age, ethnicity, gender, class and politics.

This had interesting implications for discourses of voluntary risk-taking. Those who felt the most vulnerable as a result of age, gender and exposure to actual or imagined bodily violence, such as Gemma, had no attraction to voluntary risk-taking at all. On the other hand, as in Oxfordshire and else-where, it was those who were successful at work (including women) who got a 'buzz' out of risk-taking. Adam has been playing hockey for a season with-out gum-shield or shin-guards ('because you love the sport, you take the risk'); and while Marie may not have quite achieved the male-erotics of surf-ing risk we mentioned in Chapter 2, her emotional 'adrenaline-rush' talk about her corporate embodiment describes her own, gendered version of edgework and heightened sense of living achieved through the 'buzz' of meeting challenges.

Rather than major gender differences in relation to an 'erotics' of edge-work, there is a significant difference, as we said earlier, from those who make vulnerability into a ritualized, privatized retreat against all-pervasive risk (often women). Gemma has little of that sense of actively crossing borders of plural rationalities - she had not undertaken Marie's experiential journey that led to her sense that 'whereas before I wasn't exposed to risk because I didn't really understand risk, and "risk" is a frightening word so you try to avoid it. Whereas now risk isn't like a "no-no" word.' Like many of the successful Coventry men we have discussed here, Marie believes she now has a 'mental toughness' that enables her to live life with a sense of agency. Marie's story, then, combines all three of the discourses and ratio-nalities to which we drew attention in Chapter 2:

- The discourse of self-improvement, emphasizing the importance of work-ing on the continuing project of self through taking risks;
- The discourse of emotional engagement drawing on a Romantic body/self ideal;
- The discourse of control, which, finally, privileges rational control over emotions and bodily responses as a valued aspect of engaging in risky activities.

Each of our interviewees developed their histories of control (or vulnerability) through a construction of Self and Other: Marie's narrative 'Other' is the male world of engineering which would not have given her the same oppor-tunities, even in the same company; Tina has her feminist 'Other', also, in 'patriarchal' asylum-seekers; Gemma in young men who may drug her and taxi drivers who may carry her off. But in most of these cases there are also 'Us' to these 'Others': for Marie, the Systems Department at Rover which did let her cross job-gender borders; for Gemma, her other young man, the boyfriend that protects her against 'Others'. In some cases – with Jason, Will and Catherine, for example – this 'Other' is much closer at hand, a liminality within the self itself. For Jason, capitalism inevitably 'cuts corners', that is the name of the game, whether in the case of BSE, GM foods or the rail system. And within this capitalism which is the 'only option', his notion of a cost benefit approach to risk ('amount you are willing to lose in order to get a benefit') is in itself a liminal, dangerous and challenging border. He and Catherine describe as their current risks whether to buy property in London, or not, in case the market crashes, and whether to buy critical injury insurance.

An important example of gender border-crossing and embracing of the 'Other' is evident in Tina's response to being out alone at night in Coventry city centre. As we have seen, virtually all of the Coventry women and some of the older men (like Mike) avoid this city risk, and many drive with their car doors locked when they go through it. Yet Tina is more worried about the risk of falling over in the city centre at night because of her impaired vision. Because she works in the city centre, with some of the very people whom others might fear as 'Other', Tina has crossed this particular local-spatial border between known and unknown. Having empathized with people who are 'depressed and violent' at work, she has absorbed this particular risk into her daily decision-making. This is still, as she says, her 'challenge'. On the other hand, increasing bodily impairment that comes with aging brings different city-centre risks to her.

Class and liminality are also a feature of these interviews. In at least four cases – Tina, Mike, Maria and Pat – a family working-class border has been crossed successfully via different routes: the welfare state, the army, the high-paying auto industry. In the case of ethnicity and liminality, the case is different, less interiorized, and more generational/familial. Here, the geographical places, spaces and borders are external and are as visible as on any map. What is less clear, however, is the way of marking the margins bio-graphically, culturally and economically, as Farid's narrative indicates. This is an age and generational factor; as both Farid and Rajah understand that there is now a national-cultural border between themselves and their children. It is these different 'liminal' positions within any one individual – of class, age, gender, cultural hybridity, geography and so on – which constitute 'the new situation of growing competition between overlapping discourses of risk' (Lidskog, 2000: 216).

6

Perceptions of Time and Place
in a 'Risk Modern' City

We do not *yet* live in a risk society, but we also no longer live *only* within the distribution conflicts of scarcity society. (Beck, 1992: 20, original emphases)

One of the more useful aspects of Ulrich Beck's work is his renovation of theories of modernity and the 'post-industrial'. Beck is not concerned with the society of spectacle and simulation of 'post-modernity'. As we saw in Chapter 1, his interest is with the scientific, economic, ecological political, and biographical uncertainties of the transition from 'industrial' (or 'class') modernity to 'risk modernity'. As Beck sees it, the 'concepts of "industrial" or "class" society' which 'revolved around the issue of how socially produced wealth could be distributed in a socially unequal and also legitimate way' now 'overlaps' with the new paradigm of risk society.

Time – its 'not yet ... but no longer' tension, its transition, hesitation and uncertainty between institutional orders of 'industrial' and 'risk' modernity – is thus at the heart of Beck's risk society thesis. As we have seen, this 'not yet/no longer' hesitation in Beck's theory is made more pointed by his tying of both 'class' and 'risk' society to issues of employment. This is not always recognized by commentators on Beck, since it is the environmental risk aspect of the thesis that has attained more rhetorical power in debate about the 'risk society'. Yet Beck himself seems quickly to forget the experiential power of that 'not yet/no longer' tension. Rather (and one often feels this is Beck as polemicist leaping ahead of the careful empirical sociologist), he bases much of the rhetorical power of *Risk Society* on the *opposition* between 'class' and 'risk' modernity.

Two things are clear from Beck's position. The first is his impatience with any lingering materialism of 'being' (as in the case of 'class immiseration'). The second is the unusual emphasis, given current tendencies towards theories of affect (as in Lash's work), on cognitive and scientific uncertainty. In this book we have wanted to indicate the importance of both affect and cognition. Thus, in Chapter 5 we emphasized the importance of 'plural rationalities' and our openness to an engagement with these as part of a process of dialogical incrementalism. But in that chapter, it became abundantly clear that while Beck's 'society of mass consumption and affluence (which can certainly move in tandem with an intensification of social antagonisms)' is a major source of concern to British people in its connection with fear of crime, it is not 'mostly [the] well educated and informed [who] are afraid' (except perhaps in relation to the material immiseration of 'the other'). Fear of crime is prevalent across all social groups, and the sign of it is taken to be, precisely, 'an intensification of social antagonisms' (Beck, 1992: 52). Further, among the more highly educated people we interviewed, 'transmission through knowledge' is *not* seen as an 'affliction' (1992: 52), as Beck describes it. Rather, it is the resource which gives them considerable confidence in the context of Beck's other emphasis on time.

Not only, then, are 'class' and 'risk' society in an 'overlapping' tension of 'not yet/no longer'. The risk economy, too, is a merging of 'formal and informal labour, employment and unemployment' time-frames. Work identities of *place* (organized around notions of 'working together in the same place') are, in key industries, being replaced by new identities in *time*, as more flexible short-contract, time-share and part-time employment identities emerge. Most importantly, the time perception of life-long full-time work is becoming fragmented, thus demanding new and individualized negotiations of the 'longue duree' narratives of one's life: mortgages, marriage and partnership relationships, projections of family biographies (via children), and so on. Risk individualization, for Beck, is a condition of *'disembedding'* (i.e. removal from historically prescribed co-ordinates of place: traditional family homes, centralized work sites, contained localities) and *'disenchantment'* (loss of faith in the normative demarcations of time: class solidarities and trade unions, the infallibility of science, the expectations of families).

But what if we suppose – as in practice Beck doesn't – that the two time-frames (of 'not yet/no longer' and of disembedding/disenchantment) are operating together in people's lives? This conjuncture may manifest itself in memory or in continuing material practices. As we have seen, for Beck, risk biographies become the only map available in everyday life, as the individualized citizen chooses between daily knowledges. Yet, these knowledges are systemically in 'conditions and decisions made elsewhere, in the television networks, the educational system, in firms, or the labour market, or in the transportation system, with general disregard of their private, biographical consequences' (Beck, 1992: 133). There is both a universalist aspect to Beck's analysis (are all 'risk-modern' cities similarly located places in relation to 'disembedding' and 'disenchantment', for example?) and a highly individualized one.

This is a problem for us theoretically as sociologists, in so far as the kind of situated 'everyday' analysis we are looking for needs to bring both 'place' and 'biography' together. In this final substantive chapter of the book, we want to bring together Beck's different temporalities, and we have deliberately chosen, as a context for our case study, a British city, Cardiff, which is supposedly part of a new 'fragmentation', a 'new regionalism' which, on the face of it, is all about the renewal of 'historically prescribed co-ordinates of place'. Lovering (1999), however, cautions against too simple an acceptance of the 'new regionalism' and imported 'sunrise industry' thesis, and gives evidence that since the collapse of coal and steel employment in the early 1980s, the Welsh economy has followed an economic trajectory very much in line with the rest of the UK. The reality is that the 'normalization of the economic landscape of Wales' (i.e. its increasing similarity with that of England) has occurred not because of industrial and organizational change but because of the national (British) state. Activities dominated by UK public spending accounted for a higher proportion of employment and GDP in Wales in the mid-1990s than any other UK region apart from Northern Ireland. Between 1981 and 1995, public administration and Defence, Health, and Social Services created, net around 50,000 new jobs in Wales. This is no less than 22 times the net contribution of manufacturing, despite the latter's renaissance (Lovering, 1999: 382).

In our British research (as represented in the previous two chapters), we were, broadly speaking, allowing Beck's 'industrial/high tech modernity' binary determine our choice of interviewees. And, initially, we saw the Cardiff interviews as offering the possibility of examining an example of the new regional fragmentation. Lovering's analysis, though, was sufficiently convincing for us to add interviewees who represented state-run administration. Thus in Cardiff, the 'newer industries' included five high-tech firms (IT, bio-tech and electronics); the other five were from the service sector (two insurance companies, the Bank of Wales, and two public sector organizations). Cardiff University's Innovation Network provided access to two further high-tech firms. It proved difficult to find people in older industries such as docks and mining. Representing older manufacturing/skilled manual occupations were interviewees from the car components industry, the chemical industry and a male printer. The remainder of the interviewee group comprised a rich social mix, ranging from a postwoman, a male former teacher in a children's home, an unemployed woman, a woman running a corner shop and a female shopkeeper selling organic foods. To what extent would time and place coordinates influence the risk biographies of interviewees in a capital of the 'new regionalism'?

Shani

Shani is 36, a housewife and shop-keeper, who had been brought from India as a child during the long wave of migration to a changing, post-war Britain. As 'western' countries emerged out of post-war recession and (explicit or implicit) 'white only' immigration policies, such migrants became part of a post-colonial order of 'multiculturalism'. Facing overt racism (particularly in the UK at the time of Shani's arrival), these migrants brought with them traditional skills and all-family working practices, sometimes associated with 'new' and 'exotic' food sold in restaurants and corner food shops.

The success of this 'migrant' trade was based on very long hours of work, and the employment of extended families (including schoolchildren) in their small shops. The corner shop, then, depended on round-the-clock all-family labour. But the object of this hard work, in the eyes of the older generation, was customarily to generate a new and 'educated' future for their children. We have already encountered this family/future-oriented narrative in Rajah from Coventry; and Cardiff, with a large population of Indian and Bangladeshi traders, has very many inhabitants in this category. To what extent are these numerically very significant British citizens now subject to Beck's condition of 'disembedding' and 'disenchantment'?

Shani's sense of her past/future biography depends on her memory of racist difficulties negotiated during this early period of her life:

To start a business 15 years ago was very, very difficult for ethnic minorities. It wasn't easy to make money [or] even a living as self-employed, because people weren't broad-minded then. That was the biggest risk at that time – to pay your mortgage and all that. Nowadays our people think it in a different way. It's sort of 'Let's start and see what happens, if it doesn't, oh well who cares?'. But ten years ago I think people used to care more because it was something you started. So you had a really good go at it and not let down anyone, yourself, or the community or the business or whatever it is.

For this woman, 'people think in a different way' now in *two* respects, one negative (and 'disenchanted' in terms of family expectations), one positive. The positive thing is that she has seen a major reduction in racism and a decline in what she calls the 'small-village' attitudes that treated her community as 'Other'. She believes that education – and particularly the natural mixing of different ethnicities within primary schools – has done a lot to improve things. The negative implication (which we found among other Indian small business people we interviewed, in Coventry and Oxford) was a deep sense of the loss of ethnic community and family values among their *own* younger generation. Shani is including her own ethnic community among the young 'who cares?' generation when she says:

[there is] family risk I think. There is no bond in families. There is no caring, no loving for generations, for back generations. The grandchildren don't seem to have any bond towards their grandparents. It is sad what you see these days. They won't be a loving community. There will be just each one thinks of themselves, rather than as a part. If you can't think of yourself as part of a family, or have the same feeling, warm feeling towards them, then you will never think of yourself as part of a country. It will be 'I'm doing it for myself', so it's 'Let's see what I can get out of this country – let's see what *I* get out of it', rather than 'What can I put it into it?' as well.

Hearing Shani speak, one is certainly reminded of Beck's discussion of individualization, with his emphasis on loss of social ties and historical context, so that:

Children no longer even know their parents' life context, much less that of their grandparents. That is to say, the temporal horizons of perception narrow more and more, until finally on the limiting case history shrinks to the (eternal) present, and everything revolves around the axis of one's personal ego and personal life. (Beck, 1992: 135)

Probably because family history and family futures are institutionalized more clearly (through, for example, arranged marriages which were a major 'risk' issue in the eyes of younger interviewees with sub-continental antecedents), this particular aspect on individualization was more marked in the talk of our Indian and other interviewees from the sub-continent. Here, Shani's concern for her adopted British moral order was negotiated via her own particular ethnic history, and this also has had an impact in crucial ways on the traditional economy of the corner shop. Shani has two very young children, and has recently decided to take the risk of giving up her shop in their best interests, to give them 'quality time'. She knows she is risking her home mortgage, because, with the shop gone, her husband is now working for a local company on a dubious and uncertain contract:

If you are working for somebody else and the job goes then you don't know what to do. Like this week, he was told that you are only going to do four days a week instead of five for the next four weeks. So that means you lose a week's wages. So for this month, where do we get the money from to pay the mortgage?

Shani's husband has entered Beck's new economy of under-employment. But this has been motivated primarily by a very particular sense within this family of the changing pace of life for their young children in today's Britain:

The media is worse. There is so much pumped into their young brains. At the age of five they are 15, sort of, because they have to mix up at school with all sorts of children I suppose ... There is not much we can do about it. It is difficult even now the mix with other cultures. It makes it difficult for them because there is one rule at home and one rule when they are with friends. They are pulled between two types of life-styles.

So the very thing which Shani has seen as a mind-broadening positive aspect of contemporary Britain – the mixing of different cultures at schools – is now also becoming a serious source of risk to her sense of control, her aspirations and increasing her anxiety for her own community's future as 'British'. And it is clear that she sees this according to 'conditions and decisions made elsewhere, in the television networks, the educational system, in firms, or the labour market' which have a 'general disregard of their private, biographical consequences' (Beck, 1992: 133).

This fear of a modern British culture of 'disembedding' and 'disenchantment' has led Shani and her husband to the traumatic act of selling the family business; and in turn this means her home could be at risk as her husband depends on 'risky under-employment'. But for Shani, her home is much more than bricks and mortar. It is the cultural tradition which she grew up in, and which she sees threatened by current British ways of life, especially materialism:

A lot of women are working now and it's *now*, life is not for living, it is for showing other people. So it is like, 'Oh, I've got so-and-so in the house'. And little children go around and they are saying the same things. So for them it is getting all materialized, everything is what you can get, what you can buy. What you can, you have. And, because that is what is happening in today's generation – I dread saying what it is going to be for the next generation, because there is going to be greed. They are not satisfied with what they have, they just want more and more and more.

It is clear that Shani is only too aware of Beck's risk modernity of 'the isola-ted mass market, not conscious of itself, and mass consumption of generi-cally designed housing, furnishings, articles of daily use' (1992: 135). Yet despite these fears, she is still very positive about being in Britain; and she does feel she has some control of things. It was her choice, she insists, to give up the shop; and she is prepared to adapt to current British ways. If her husband loses her job, she will go back to work, but it will be different work. Her Indian family shop-keeping tradition is over. She recognizes the need to be 'up-to-date and mobile'. On the one hand, she would have to draw on her tradition (of family support for her children) in those circumstances. But on the other hand, she will be looking for 'a good job', obtained after studying for further qualifications at college.

Shani intends, as far as she is able, to become part of Cardiff's 'knowledge economy'. This perceptual move towards the 'new economy' is also moti-vated by her sense of her changing (small shop) workplace in her locality. She is cognisant of the changes around her in Canton, her suburb of Cardiff, where huge new supermarkets have opened (the new Tescos supermarket being so big that staff move around on roller-blades!). So Shani speaks of her 'most recent feeling of risk' as 'with supermarkets opening up on every corner, corner shops were going down. It was making it very, very difficult for corner shop people to survive'.

Though Shani blames the local council for not supporting small business people, and the media for saying nothing at all about their plight, she is still determined to be positive about her adopted country. Her positive view of living in Britain is evident in her response to the Paddington rail crash. As still very much a 'local' person, she is not as yet very mobile:

Compared to other countries, over here everything here is so good. All the facilities are brilliant. When you compare it with other countries I think we should be grateful, not always point out 'Oh there was a plane crash, it was someone's fault'. Why don't you think about that there are so many thousands of planes coming in, every second coming in and out of Heathrow and not all of them have accidents? It is one of those things that has to happen.

There is no sensed connection here of what Beck calls the 'unchanged logic of profit-oriented rationalization' (1992: 149) between Shani's husband's 'risky underemployment' and the demonstrated lack of infrastructural safety measures that led to the Paddington rail crash. Similarly, in the case of GM food, she has no knowledge or concern about it. 'Unless I know what it is all about, I can't say that it is a risk. You have to have all the facts in front of you. So if I don't know anything about it I can't say it is risky.'

Shani's sense of risk 'disenchantment' then, does not reach out into an uncertain future of technology and scientific change. Rather, her fears for the

111

future of her children are primarily as an extrapolation from her own past cultural traditions. But Shani, too, is located in a 'not yet/no longer' situation. It is a migrant inflection of the one that Beck describes. She is trying to adapt to a new national, cultural and knowledge economy order. But some things about the mix of cultures haunt her as she speculates on time and the future of her children. Similarly, the opening of supermarkets is killing the sense of local place and community:

> Corner shops, post offices – they were all sort of meeting points for a lot of people, so they were separate. You go to a supermarket and nobody stands there talking to you. But when you go to these little shops, you do stand there, you do spend some time with people, you do mix up with other people living in the area. If you don't come into the village then you lose out on that as well.

We should remember – as Beck does not – that in the risk society of 'mass consumption of generically designed housing, furnishings, articles of daily use' (1992: 135), by no means all places of work are becoming less concentrated. Beck thinks of factories too much, supermarkets too little. These are by no means becoming 'invisible'. Rather, it is the corner shops – and the resources of 'talking' with customers there – that are becoming fragmented and invisible. What was once the small-minded centre of anti-Indian racism – 'the village' (which is how Shani describes her Cardiff suburb) – is now a memory of multicultural community where 'you mix and talk' with other kinds of people living in your area. But she recognizes that this community is in the (for her, recent) past. And presumably, it is people from this same community who threaten (via media influence) the pace and timing of change for her young children.

Karen

Karen, 33, is also a shop-keeper. Like Shani, Karen has an Indian cultural connection, in this case through her husband Neil. Neil's parents emigrated from India to the UK when he was a child. His father was qualified in medicine and was able to practice as a doctor after his arrival. This was a different class background from Shani's Indian family; and now that Neil's parents are dead, an inheritance from them (plus savings from earlier jobs schoolteaching) have enabled Karen and Neil to start an organic food shop in Penarth. This is an affluent coastal suburb (that was originally the home of Cardiff's coal-shipping magnates) which still has 'local village' self-identities.

While Karen and Neil recognized the risk in giving up permanent teaching jobs, they owe nothing to the bank for their business – a sign (and effect) of the economic 'independence' instilled and bequeathed by Neil's doctor father. As a precaution (because of the local supermarkets' recent turn to organic food) Karen keeps her hand in by doing some supply teaching; and she reminds herself when anxious about supermarket competition that both she and her husband have science-teaching qualifications. Penarth is a popular and attractive area for 'new economy' professionals who are moving to

Cardiff from London and other insurance and banking centres. Consequently, 'high quality' schools are expanding there; and Karen foresees little difficulty in getting back into local teaching if necessary.

Like Shani, Karen has a very strong feeling about her local 'community', and she too, fears its passing. She, too, speaks about a growing breakdown in social relationships and a turn towards materialism and egocentrism:

> We are becoming less social and more selfish: 'I want it so I will have it. I want it this way so I will have it this way'. People that come into our shop – and lots and lots of people have said this – they miss the old community that supermarkets took away to a certain extent.

Like Shani also, Karen has a strong sense of risk and disenchantment associated with time (life is 'speeding up too much') and place (the over-crowded nature of Britain). She worries about all the road rage, aggressiveness and selfishness this seems to be creating, which she sees spreading even to children in the streets of Penarth. Karen, too, thoroughly regrets the disembedded removal 'from historically prescribed social forms and commitments in the sense of traditional contexts of dominance and support under new conditions of market mobility' (Beck, 1992: 128). Clearly, she prefers (at least in her distanced perception) the more traditional 'tolerance from one individual to the next' that she sees in the more traditional cultures of India. And via her organic food shop, she sees some minor replication of this in her 'village' of Penarth.

Unlike Shani – also a food shop-keeper – Karen is thoroughly 'in' to the ecological and environmental movement, 'doing her bit' by keeping the organic food shop going. She worries about environmental risk both locally and globally: 'I don't know if it comes with our work really, because it is an organic shop – but lots of the conversations you have seem to be gloom-and-doom about pesticides and the agricultural age in intensive farming. So it is things like that [we talk about] – things like radiation in the environment.' Karen is very clearly one of Beck's 'better educated' people, who 'actively inform themselves' in risk society; and who (like Beck) worry especially about the 'invisibility' of environmental risk (her particular concern is about 'radiation in the environment'). Beck argues that this 'type of [knowledge] affliction produces no social unity that would be visible on its own and to others', but in fact it is clear that Karen and Neil do have a strong sense of social unity with the customers of their 'village' shop.

Karen and Neil are middle-class people, owing nothing to the bank, who can afford to be 'new age' in their sense of place and local identity. It is the *informal* community within their shop – the talk with customers 'about pesticides and the agricultural age in intensive farming' – which produces Karen's 're-embedding' and sense of new social commitments. If she has any sense of control or 'reintegration' in the context of perceived 'materialism', job change, rapid time shifts and local 'breakdown', it comes from here (and the informal 'sub-politics' of risk organized around organic food), and not from the media.

Despite the fact that the mass media has strongly condemned GM food in Britain, Karen does not trust TV or newspapers because (like Beck) she finds they work in 'short-term' fashions, rather than systematically. Instead, she relies for her information on two other sources of communication: specialist magazines, and the 'village' community in Penarth (of which she sees her organic shop as a 'reintegrating' centre). As she and her husband are both science-trained, they are deeply suspicious of science 'experts' and their connections in the GM debate:

> As scientists, you realize that you can manipulate statistics. If a certain person wants you to come up with certain results, you can get them if you want ... That is the whole crux of the matter. Whoever they are working for they want to try and please, because then scientists go from contract to contract and they want to come up with the right results.

Karen and her husband are perfectly aware of the new 'short contract' economy, and of scientists' non-neutral affiliations within it. These are very clearly Beck's risk citizens whose 'consciousness (knowledge) determines being' (1992: 53). They are deeply suspicious of governments who have become, in their view, ever more closely implicated with big business. Thus it is not the mass (new or old) media, or 'experts', or even the schooling system that they were trained for that Karen and Neil are mobilizing in negotiating risk. Rather, they are mobilizing resources and circuits of communication 'in the shop' to avoid (experts') 'information overload'.

At the time of interview Karen was pregnant with her first child. Like Shani, she worries greatly about the world her child will grow up in, ranging from the invisible risks from science and technology which she feels she can do nothing about, to the increasing aggression shown by children at school and young people on the road. The previous week a boy she had once taught sat next to her on the bus in 'leafy Penarth' and showed her property he had stolen, talking loudly for everybody to hear. She was particularly shocked that this could happen, so brazenly, 'even in Penarth'.

Consequently, Karen's sense of the relationship between her *personal* past/present and a broader sense of *place* (her workplace, her local community, her sense of being in an overcrowded national community) begins with fears of environmental risk, but goes well beyond that. Living in Penarth, Wales, is but a microcosm of a national (indeed global) risk society:

> Like this thing on the news last night, did you see – the Philippines, this rubbish tip crashing down on this shanty town and killing hundreds? It was disgusting the pictures – these people who live off the tip, salvaging bits of rubbish. You can imagine a landfill falling on a shanty town: oh, it was just foul! But, you know, I worry that is almost like a metaphor for the world in a way. In that we try and pile it all in a corner, but it will come back in the end. So yes, overpopulation brings a lot of problems with it, lots of risks to the individual.

Karen brings places like the Philippines home, as metaphors which make her own over-crowded island place seem even more dangerous as time passes. Like many interviewees we interviewed in British cities, the sense of over-crowding (and with it the risk of travelling about) was very strong indeed. Now that she is pregnant, she is trying to: 'think for two – more long term. I do think about the future of the world that the baby is coming into, and the risk that the baby will face. And if I recognize them now, I can maybe somehow help my child face them when he or she has to face them.'

But the trouble is, Karen says, in the midst of all this 'information over-load', 'People haven't got the information that they need to live their lives. Whereas they know so much else, and they worry about so much else.' Public institutions do not help. The media 'can do a lot of damage and they can influence by the power of suggestion'. She is dismayed by a media that concentrates attention on the '20 to 30-somethings, with very little tolerance of children and the elderly'. Feeling disenfranchized politically, threatened locally, and bombarded by an overload of the 'wrong' information, Karen has to dig deep for Neil's father's 'independence', relying substantially for the 'information needed' on the informal 'voices' that cluster in her organic shop in Penarth.

Both of our first two case studies are people who have been working in 'traditional' sectors of the economy. Both are women. Both are about the same age and they have some similar ethnic connections. But they are different in class, and they are different in their local 'place'. Though Shani's suburb of Canton is becoming increasingly middle-class (like Penarth, it has become a popular place of residence for university teachers and other young professionals), it also edges on to the main concentration of Indian and Bangladeshi communities in Cardiff. Karen's 'leafy Penarth' has no visible non-white community at all. As we have seen, different aspirations of place and expectations of time are negotiated by two traditional workers who have many other perceptions of Britain's 'disembedded' society in common.

Jean

Jean, 49, works as an official for the European Commission. Unlike Shani and Karen, this 'knowledge economy' professional woman does not worry too much about the future direction of British society and culture, holding a generally optimistic view.

Jean is far more specific in her sense of *regional* (devolved, Welsh) place and risk than Shani or Karen. She is one of Lovering's many new 'state' professionals who is responsible for the regeneration of Cardiff, and thus may be seen as symptomatic (despite her 'Welsh-based' rhetoric) of its place in the globalized economy. Certainly, Jean is part of the 'knowledge economy' rhetoric through which Cardiff self-profiles its 'post-industrial' status. Thus Jean – no less aware than Shani or Karen of continuing risks for British people – articulates these in relation to 'the people on the wrong side of clever' (which is where she positions Karen's sense of political disenfranchisement), or 'in other words allowing short-term emotional personal

115

responses to overtake them, either as a controlling factor in decisions about attitudes and values, or in political choices that they make.' Jean goes on to list the risks she sees as threatening British people:

> In economic terms, I think the biggest risk to people is loss of job, loss of house, loss of health, loss of mobility, loss of status, loss of quality of life, and I think that there is this threat of complete abandonment. There is quite a sense, I think, of this change in the labour force, where the increase in risk, in terms of security of tenure and job contracts and so on, has given rise to 'there but for the grace of God go I'. There is an increasing lack of control by people for their own sense of wellbeing. In personal terms you see people taking up a lot more risky hobbies. You see people taking personal risk because of the increase in this kind of search for material wellbeing, rather than personal or private wellbeing. And socially, I think, there is a real risk of people finding themselves outside, alone, without support.

Like nearly all of our Cardiff interviewees in the 'new economy' sector, Jean is reflexive about what Beck describes as the shift from the (welfare) society of 'goods', to the (risk) society of 'bads' (which depends so fundamentally on short contracts and the end of 'a job for life'). Clearly, though, she links these 'bads' (as a residual category) to the *'perception* of risk' among 'the people on the wrong side of clever'. A recurring trope in the risk biographies and future expectations of these 'new economy' interviewees is their *own* sense of comfort and adaptation in this new world of risk.

Jean, though, is unusually personalizing and biographical in her account. According to her 'half-way objective assessment', she is a multiple risk-taker (in her car, going out alone at night, climbing mountains in her leisure time), but she is not one of the 'wrong side of clever' victims of risk (she would certainly disagree with Beck's view that today's victims of risk are people with knowledge, like herself). There are, Jean believes, two reasons for this: one personal/biographical; the other social and political.

Personally, Jean defines herself as of the 'warrior class'. Her discursive relationship with her personal past is not with family traditions and values (as it was with Shani and Karen). Rather, it is with the long-term temporality of herself as a long-term street-wise and cognitive risk-taker, starting from when she was a young girl:

> All my life, I cannot remember not knowing about risk, because if you don't take risks there is no movement, there is no change. It doesn't have to be progress; it doesn't need to be positive. But I am not always terribly happy with things at a standing state or at a state of inertia, and if you change things, if you move things, if you affect things then that involves risk ... I risk by being controversial. I risk by being challenging. I risk by being outspoken. I risk by being a woman. I risk by being searching and seeking out areas where consensus is not what we are looking at, but rather areas where the plates aren't sliding easily together, where there might be fractures and faults. Because that is the most interesting bit, and that is also the bit that needs work.

Jean's is a confident personal biography of risk-identity, beginning at the time she 'went to a number of schools as a child and risked expulsion'. It juxtaposes and engages two things: on the one hand, the personal-biographical 'risk competence' where you 'understand it, know about it, calculate it and judge your involvement and the extent you participate with the risk factor';

on the other hand, the 'fractures and faults' of a new social order. Crucially, also, this personalized risk biography is defined against continuing generations of people who are not 'challenging':

> I think that the old idea of being radical when you are young and more conservative as you get older is being turned on its head. I see that the way threats and risks are perceived now, the way they are relayed in the media, through the education system, through the family networks means that people take fewer risks from an even younger age. That there is this culture of trying to increase your security levels because of the increased intolerance of risk-taking, especially in the increased tolerance of failure. That means that people generally are actually taking less risks earlier, and the only people who can afford to take risks are the older people whose emotional, personal and economic security is already in the bag.

Jean is clearly a Beck-like thinker, in so far as she describes Britain as a society where people are finding their identities – positively (like her) or negatively – in risk. She is also like Beck – and this is the second reason for her optimism over not being a 'risk victim' – recognizing the proliferation of a new sub-politics:

> There has been this increase in awareness by small groups, by individuals, of the power they have, both political and personal in affecting these things. So, you could look to the environmental movement or the women's movement or the anti-racist movements, the anti-Nazi movements, whatever, for people taking a lot more spontaneous political response. And therefore whatever action they took has in a way reduced risks. Even the CND, the anti-nuclear campaign, which became the only political campaign in the '50s, was about reducing risk and people suddenly realized their powerfulness.

In her view, people have a greater *perception* of risk in Britain today, and therefore a greater *engagement* with it:

> If you are in the warrior class you take risks relentlessly. But also I am somebody who is not without fear, but who thinks of themselves as having every right to pursue a line or an action that as long it isn't risking other people's wellbeing, and can be justified to myself, I will pursue it, and that puts me at risk.

This is Beck's new 'individualizing' generation 'opening up possibilities to choose' (2000a: 105), in which Karen places her beliefs. She is, to a degree, 'disenchanted' with science. As a science-trained professional, she is cautious about any scientific logic or 'data'. As for the GM food debate:

> I certainly don't believe that an emotional response will necessarily be wrong just because it isn't based on facts that we don't know. Because the whole point about scientific knowledge is not what you know, it is about what you don't know. And we don't know a hell of a lot about all this. So, I don't believe that one particular theoretical test result, one experimental result tells us any more than just one small incremental change, and that could be turned upside down by another experiment somewhere else repeated on exactly the same basis. So, I don't believe anybody, I just monitor it.

On the other hand though, Karen is positive about what scientific knowledge and developments can offer humankind, against which concerns about GM food pale into insignificance:

> The biological revolution since the '50s with our increased knowledge of biochemistry – particularly that of the genes that make up human and plant and other animal life – is a phenomenal

117

revolution. I mean, when Darwin wrote *Evolution of the Species* and anticipated all this, nobody could predict that today it was announced as the mapping of the human gene. I have to say, personally, that I see GM food as a very, very low risk in my life and even if the outcome was horrific, because I don't have children the risk to me personally is very, very limited. I am unlikely to eat a soya-bean plant that has been genetically modified and for it to have any direct effect on me.

Jean, unlike Shani and Karen, does not project a dystopian future – either personally via children, or socially via 'science'. She is confident, as 'warrior' and cognitive risk-taker, to 'just monitor it'. She is, in fact, one of Beck's new scientist-citizens, aware of the intra-cultural divisions and uncertainties within sciences, yet confident enough in her 'official' role to be her own expert:

Experts? I have learnt more from other people. I have learnt more from personal behaviour and judging the risks [I have taken], and watching others and how they have judged risk-taking, and from watching other people succeed in terms of reducing risk. Even if it was just risk of poverty, I would watch how somebody avoided that. No, I don't take much notice of experts, although my sense of environmental risk was through my studies. I did science, so my estimation of risk and hazards has a scientific basis. But because risk is very much to do with perception, if I know somebody well enough, I can strip away the personal imprint that they make in their risk assessment. But if I only take on the views of either what you call a professional or statistical or media or some other expert, I don't have that additional information that allows me to make a more accurate calculation. I think it is more plausible to base your risk on real-life examples, complemented by looking at means and medians of results, rather than *starting* with the means and the medians and then looking at your own situation as a test.

Her biography of risk ('real life examples') has made Jean socially confident. But her social and educational confidence (in speaking about 'means and medians') has retrospectively vindicated her personal biography. Thus Jean does not feel the need to lay blame on governments, nor on corporations. She prefers to move on biographically (and powerfully) with her risk identity, until she gets to be called 'barmy'. Consequently, she is not in the least bit nervous about train travel after the Paddington crash:

There are so many trains travelling, so many old trains with old stock travelling on old poorly maintained track with so little investment over such a long period with such poor professional training and other standards and checks for crew and staff involved that I wasn't at all surprised. I mean, it is just a statistical likelihood that was totally predictable.

To have 'laid blame' (on corporate or government inaction and greed) would have seemed to Jean to be too much part of an older 'enchanted' social order. Rather, she seeks to 'go on' with her warrior-project: the risk biography of 'choice'.

Jean is equally sanguine and 'individualized' about GM food. Its debate is just another part of the longue duree of her own (controlled) biography. 'Oh, I have known about it forever because I did bio-chemistry at university, and I have known about genetic modification since I was at school.' Rather than blame governments for lack of rail investment, or suspect big business in relation to GM food research, she emphasizes a 'warrior' responsibility: a matter of choice in the risk society:

I am not very strong on blame. I am much more inclined to responsibility. I mean, that involves each and every one of us, because risk is in *everyday* actions, as I say. It could be whether I decide to jump on a bus whilst it is moving – that is a risk and who is responsible for that? That's me, but if I get run over by the bus because I am jay walking, is it the bus driver or is it me? I mean these are all shared, just as even if I live near a factory that sends out poisonous fumes, there is still a decision that I have made to live there and I could move. Any decision involves risks, because it can be more or less a good decision. And that can be anything from what sandwich to choose and whether it is a day over its sell-by date. Then you risk getting salmonella poisoning because you have saved yourself 60p, and who is responsible there? Is it them selling it to you, or is it you as a consumer? It is a balance.

This confidence (among all ages and regions) of our 'new economy' interviewees is their most common and symptomatic feature. Virtually all of them self-describe as risk-takers in what they all define as a risk society, as we will see in the following case study of two much younger 'high-tech' men.

Justin and Cameron

Justin, 27, and Cameron, 28, both have university degrees and work in small (but at the time of interview, very successful) high-tech firms. Like Jean, Justin was not a 'good' school student, and nor did he do well at university. But in the short time since leaving formal education, he has taken financial risks and thus far has flourished. His major risk, he describes, is having given up a well-paid job in the south of England to 'move home' to Wales, where he set up his own IT company.

Justin has a reflexive sense of past/present family biography. He compares his own situation of successful mobility with the more desperate mobility of his parents, whom he sees as trapped in a very different economic system:

This moving away from home thing is one thing that did happen to my own family. My parents are from up-north in Lancashire and I think it was quite a big thing for them to move out of the family unit. My dad moved down to London, and that was quite a big thing in the '60s and '50s. It was simply because up in Lancashire at the time it was a dead industry in terms of linen and cotton. That was their main industry; it just went and so they just had to look out for work elsewhere.

His own situation is much more fortunate, since the industrial concentrations and confines of 'place' have been breached:

I think technology is becoming more accessible in terms of things like the Internet. I think probably there are more opportunities now. Britain is not reliant on minerals and things like that to make its money. It can look at alternative technologies, which is obviously exciting.

But Justin is also *professionally* reflexive, in so far as he is aware of the possibilities of his good fortune and risk enterprise 'turning pear shaped'. This is on a number of counts: competition is fierce ('it is an easy industry to get in to'); the specific technology he works with may become less fashionable ('Just the risk that it could all go wrong tomorrow. All of a sudden they could find that the Internet kills babies or something and hey presto, it is gone. Funnier things have happened.'); the UK is, in his opinion, too tribal (e.g.

119

football hooliganism) and insular. Countries like France have caught up and Britain could get left behind on the 'technological super-highway'; there is also too much intra-regional rivalry (e.g. Northern Ireland) and not enough 'macro-thinking' (there is a need to think 'beyond Wales', to set up international partnerships, etc.).

But thus far Justin is confident in both his regional and his national location. In Cardiff, he has recently won a major IT contract with Cardiff University, and Britain is still well-positioned in the new technology field. Like many other high-tech and IT interviewees we interviewed, he is very confident about the marketability of his 'new knowledge'. He argues that if the worst happened to his business, he could always get paid 'ridiculous amounts of money' for very short-contract work with other IT companies.

In addition to these personal, local and national competence advantages, Justin also believes his management practices stand him in good stead in terms of future possibilities. He never bad-mouths competitors. He always treats well those colleagues who leave his company (aware that they may well go to work for competitors or clients). He takes advice, from clients as well as from expert bodies. He employs like-minded people who work hard for the organization, and have a shared sense of ownership.

Life is very much better for Justin now than ten years previously, when he was doing poorly academically. He has a fast car (and takes risks in it). He has a stable relationship (and would not take risks sexually). He has good health (he has given up smoking). Like a number of our high-tech interviewees, he extends his business risk-taking into the leisure field, liking to take 'controlled' recreational risks while mountain biking and diving. He admits also to 'soft risks', like losing touch with his family. But unlike earlier Cardiff interviewees like Shani and Karen, he is not especially worried about these looser ties since family traditions have as many minuses as pluses. He has *chosen* to be 'disembedded' in what Beck calls 'the "liberating" dimension' (1992: 128), free from the ascribed class fixity of his parents, under new conditions of choice and market mobility, away from familial traditions, and also away from the geographical centralization of the 'visible' work site.

Justin is not anxious about the future, believing he has the right professional skills and adaptability for the new economy. Change is a feature of this economy and he does not lose sleep worrying about where it is all going. In terms of long-term issues like GM food, his response is also similar to other high-tech interviewees in Oxford and Coventry. Like Jean, he feels confident to stay on the sideline and 'just monitor':

> I think I am quite good at remaining on the sideline of things. With reference to GM food crops, part of me patently hates them and disagrees with them and thinks they are really bad and can do lots of damage because it is the unknown, dabbling with nature and all the rest of it. But, on the other hand as a scientist, part of me thinks it is brilliant, it is good, it is going to stop stuff rotting. It means stuff is going to last longer. It means we don't have to use so much pesticide and will grow natural products. So I think there are benefits and disadvantages.

Risk, for Justin, 'is not an on/off thing. It is not a binary thing'. He does tend to reach for organic food on the supermarket shelves. But this is more because of the danger of pesticides than from fear for an ongoing genetic threat to humankind. His responses are practical and contingent, rather than philosophical and future-predictive:

> Scientists don't necessarily know all the answers from day one, and smoking is a perfect example. It was only 20 years ago that they realized that it does cause cancer. What if these chemicals and pesticides which are supposedly safe now, what if in 20 years time or 50 years time or 100 years time the damage is done? There is not a lot you can do.

While certainly not being blind to the future risks of science and technology, Justin is much more focused on the 'just-in-time' present (hence he has given up smoking, but doesn't worry too much about GM food). This current time-frame is both in comparison with the Britain of his parents, and in terms of sharp, continuing disparities in wealth between the knowledge rich and the information poor. Like Jean – and other young high-tech interviewees we interviewed in Oxford and Coventry – our two Cardiff high-tech interviewees seem some way from being the selfish, '20s to 30s something' 'me' generation that older, more traditionally employed people worried about. Certainly they self-describe as part of the young 'I want' generation that Shani and Karen deplore. But they are also reflexive, both about their good fortune (generationally), and about the negative 'other' side of the society whose economy they were driving.

Here is Justin speaking about call centres in Wales, which are a focus of official rhetoric about Wales' success in attracting financial and business services' investments:

> In Wales these call centres are springing up, like the Bank Royal. And the reason they are located in these areas is because they don't have to pay people very much. If they are to build a call centre with 100 people working down in the south of England it would cost a lot more. So they come to areas where there are millions of people looking for work, such as Wales and Ireland. Hence all these big call centres are set up in these areas. Which is good, I suppose, because at the end of the day it gets employment down. But it is bad because people do get victimized, and maybe effectively get paid less than they should be.

Cameron is less ambivalent in his criticism of his chosen region. But his historical analysis about the decline of wages and employment in Wales is also an elaboration of Justin's reflections on his own parents' experience of Lancashire. For Cameron, decline in Welsh wages…

> comes from the predominant decline in traditional industry. When the traditional industries go, when the factories go and the steelworks go and the mines go and the pits go and the shipbuilding yards go, then you get displaced populations, and those that stay remain unemployed and those that want to work move. So, that is basically where it comes from.

Cameron, Justin and virtually every other high-tech interviewee were clear about there now being two kinds of work culture; and that one of them is 'going to the wall', leading to alienation, crime, poverty, ill-health and hardship of all kinds. Like Jean, Cameron describes a 'victim culture':

The young are possibly at risk, young women especially. Not through physical violence or anything, but I think there is something wrong with the social make-up that allows so many women to get pregnant as teenagers. It allows so many people to slip through the education nets, and so many people to slip into drug abuse and things like that. That's the problem with society itself. It's probably also part of the British make-up: a 'victim culture' if you like. I think a lot of people – if you come from families where parents are unemployed and possibly where aunts and uncles and extended family members are unemployed as well – have such a low self-esteem that they drift into parenthood and drug abuse and alcohol abuse, when something should be done to stop it. I don't know what can be done. There is no obvious solution.

The very same mobility which is a positive part of the high-tech interviewees' sense of being 'on top of their game' (like Justin, Cameron left a secure job in England to join an IT company in Cardiff), is seen as an enforced curse and hardship for this 'other' Britain. Cameron talks about life becoming more stressful for many people because of 'the instability of jobs and also the breakdown of the traditional extended family'. Crucial to this high-tech theory of 'two nations' is Cameron's point that:

Certainly for employment, the culture of a job for life has gone. Now for someone who has never really been involved in that, that's no great shock. But I would imagine for somebody losing their job in their 40s or early 50s, that would be a massive thing for them. And that's increasing all the time and will continue to increase, I think. Work-wise they have to be prepared for the fact that they are going to change a job a number of times during their careers, maybe a number of times during a year.

In contrast to this 'other' Britain, Cameron feels reasonably in control of his life. He has lived with his partner for five years and is about to get married, with a baby on the way. Like Justin, he has a direct and collegial input into the management and future planning of the small IT company that he works for. He has (unlike Justin) given up physical sports because he cannot afford the lay-off from work that a broken arm would bring. He feels he is past the sexual and other experimentations of ten years earlier, and, with a family starting, 'wouldn't dream of being unfaithful'.

Cameron does see risks associated with his work. But, again, he articulates these (positively) in the context of the 'other' Britain.

Risk of unemployment in a lot of areas is still massive, especially in traditional industries because of the pound being too strong, Britain's reluctance to join the Euro. All of these things are going to be detrimental to the British economy, which means it is going to be detrimental to people ... I think for people in manufacturing – but also I guess for people in high-tech as well to a certain extent – you do have more problems selling your goods abroad than you would do if the pound were lower. Fortunately, I think at the moment, there aren't enough high quality service providers or high quality firms around for the amount of high-tech stuff that is required in Britain. So at the moment I would say that the high-tech industries – not necessarily high-tech manufacturing but certainly high-tech service-provision industries – are fairly safe.

In contrast to workers in 'traditional industries', Cameron does feel adapted to the new economy. For example, he is buying his first house in time for his upcoming wedding (signing the contract the day after the interview). He acknowledges that with himself in a small company competing in an aggressive field, and his wife working on short-term contracts, there could be a problem with the mortgage down the line. But short-term contracts are 'the future now'. So you 'either go with it and buy your house' in this new situation, or you never do. Cameron has the confidence to go with it, as does every other young high-tech professional we interviewed.

Cameron's attitude to the GM food debate is similar to Justin's: he is in two minds. On the one hand he worries about local environmental effects, but on the other he admires the possibility of science alleviating the problem of mass food production on a global scale. Like many other young high-tech workers we interviewed, his use of the media here is 'discriminating' and confident. On the GM issue he turns to the *New Scientist*, on other specific issues to the *Internationalist*, and for more general information to broadsheets like the *Guardian*.

We didn't ask any of our interviewees about their political voting preferences. But there is no doubt that in the high-tech hinterlands of Oxfordshire, Coventry and Cardiff, with their mix of optimism in a 'clever country' and their (somewhat pessimistic) social conscience, there were many potential constituents of New Labour. Cameron was perhaps unusual (but not alone among our high-tech interviewees) in being a little to the left of that, apologizing from time to time for 'sounding a bit Marxist'. So though he was 'statistically' unperturbed (like Jean and Justin) by the Paddington rail crash, he also advocated some form of re-nationalization:

> The government doesn't invest enough money on our public transport systems and never has done. I think that the government gave [the private rail companies] too much power over something that they weren't qualified to do. I don't know how many different rail companies we've got working in Britain (15 or 20 I would guess), different rail companies that have different regulations and they have got the interest of their shareholders at heart. I think that the government does have the power to take it back. I think they should do.

From this left-leaning, young high-tech professional, we will move to a case study of the industries which Cameron describes as 'at terrible risk', where we will find another left-leaning worker of Cameron's age.

Rick and Glyn

This case study contrasts two men from the 'other' Britain of traditional industry. They differ also between themselves: in age, employment seniority and unionization. Rick is a 28-year-old printer. As a union leader, he has a strong sense of his working past, starting work as an apprentice in the Thatcher years. If Shani's sense of 'disenchantment' is in 'the loss of traditional security' with respect to the practical knowledge, faith and guiding norms (Beck, 1992: 128) of familial expectations, Rick's is in the loss of class solidarities conveyed by strong trade unions. His memories are of 'the print union as probably the last of the strongest unions, one of them. It is gradually crumbling away. The factory where I work in is where there used to be what they call a "closed shop", where if you weren't a union member you couldn't work there, it was as simple as that.'

123

As an apprentice, he watched as Thatcher (and Murdoch) destroyed the strongest unions. Thus, 'choice', for Rick, does not mean the same, positive thing as it does to Jean. 'You have now got the choice [to join the union], and to deny somebody the choice not to is "being unfair to them", which brings up the whole discrimination and what have you. There's not too much you can't do nowadays.'

His unionism is still important to him, as some (much diminished) means of moderating management's power:

> because a lot of places don't have a union any more and it's just you against the management then. So if anything happens, say you do get wrongly accused of something, you are up the creek and you have got no back-up or anything, whereas the union will and can step in to argue your case. It does carry a bit more weight. Because in a lot of your little cases where you are just the one person and they can just say, 'You're fired', or whatever and that is the end of it, whereas the union can make quite a bit of a noise about it if they really want to.

This is a young man living off the residues of a different 'class/industrial' past, relaying on the remembered voices of older men that he met in that different modernity when he began work as a printer. He is not always sure those past voices were altogether right. Like another unionist we interviewed in Coventry, he acknowledges that there are stricter regulations now, and talks in detail about the chemical risks that they accepted in those days, because of the high wages they earned. But, whether right or wrong, those 'class' voices from his working past are important to him. They are resources mediating the relationship between his personal past and his present sense of place. He is very aware of the impoverishment of the workplace that their disappearance has left with him.

For example, like some high-tech interviewees, he talks about the problem of house mortgages. But he worries in a very different way. For Rick, this is his 'biggest risk', because, unlike the high-tech professionals, he does not have the same sense of control of his fate through currently marketable skills. As a unionist he does his best to protect his own and others' jobs:

> I am the union rep up there, so I talk with management quite a bit. You've constantly got to argue your case because we've got what we call a house agreement up there which is a like a code of practice, from manning levels, to sickness, to holidays, to whatever basically. And management being management, is always trying to cut corners and maybe not lay on the right staff etc., just try and pull a stunt. And then you have just got to constantly go in waving that, and saying 'You can't do this', and then argue it off.

But, as the representative of a weakened union, Rick can do little more to protect his own job than 'not messing up' at the individual level:

> I can control it to a degree whereas as long as I don't mess up, or do anything silly in work, I'll be all right. But it reaches a line when like at the moment there is not a lot of work on, and then obviously the rumours start flying about that there could be closures, there could be redundancies and those sort of things. You have just got to sit back and wait for it to happen really.

In this context, Rick may try to mobilize very different 'economic' skills from Justin and Cameron. He hints in the interview about shoplifting, and mentions that one of his mates has gone to prison. Basically, he blames New Labour for not helping the working class:

It's the knock-on effect. You lose your job. Then you lose your house. And if you don't do anything about it, or if you are in the situation where you can't do anything about it – like so many places up north and up the Welsh valleys, Merthyr and all that, they've got hardly anything up there – it is total change. That's been especially [obvious] since I've lived down here [in Wales] with what we've all got on our doorstep.

Unlike Justin, Rick's move back to Wales has given him a greater sense of risk. The 'knock-on effect' is a description of time, place and causality out of individual or collective control. In this situation, he also blames the government for letting in 'too many migrants' whom he believes take workers' jobs:

What pisses me off is that we have got enough homeless people of our own, sort of thing. I know we have been welcoming people in for years and years due to whatever reasons. But I think there has got to be a time when you say, 'Look, sorry we can't have any more for the moment. We have got enough problems of our own'. It's like the government want to help people outside of Britain, but couldn't give a fuck about their own.

He blames the government also – and the rail companies – for the Paddington rail crash. As a unionist, he rejects privatization and corporate control of public services:

They have taken so much money out of it. It's the same with the air traffic controllers, they are trying to privatize that. Now to me, if there's a major disaster you can say, 'Right this is underfunded, but this is run by government, so therefore somebody is accountable for it'. But if you privatize it, it is all different little corporations and people can hide away. They will be hidden away a lot easier if something does go wrong.

As for GM food, Rick has got too many other current worries to bother about it too much. It is a distant future:

I think a lot of what we are eating anyway has been like it for a while. Tomatoes and what have you, they all have something put in them to give them a longer shelf life. I think where they are now they have taken it another step on, haven't they? Rather than just vegetables, they want to go on to genetically modifying sheep and livestock. We are all just guinea pigs.

Rick has experienced Thatcher's use of workers as guinea pigs. GM food is a much lesser evil for him.

Glyn is much older than Rick, a 49-year-old production-team manager in a car components company. Unlike Rick, he is 'middle-management' and so is not unionized. Which means that he has even less say in protecting his job than Rick does:

It is getting harder to make ends meet, to survive, to keep your job down. Will I have a job tomorrow, next month, next year? Are they going to continue to employ me doing the job that I am doing? Am I going to be doing something else? You never know. With the business that we are in, and the current climate within the industry, it is always a threat. I mean, right now I'm comfortable, but six months down the road all that could change.

Glyn also has major problems with his marriage. His wife has been seriously depressed, and Glyn (rather elusively) says it is to do with having to deal with three men in the house (he has two university-age sons) and with her 'time of life'. Additionally, his mother has been in hospital recently with a very severe stroke, and he worries whether his father can cope when she comes home. But there is nothing – financially or emotionally – he feels he can do. His resources are minimal.

In the case of his wife's depression, Glyn did get helpful advice from his GP, and a mate cut out a piece on Prozac and depression from the newspaper. He worries that losing his job will mean not being able to keep his sons at university and thus break the cycle for them that he is trapped in. He doesn't give a second thought to the GM issue; and was not the least surprised about the Paddington rail crash. As at his place of work, 'where there was two people doing a job there is now one and the pressures are on'. So it was an accident waiting to happen – like the rest of his own life.

Almost entirely, Glyn's life is determined by 'other people that have other influences and other thoughts'. His is the ultimate 'risk society', with 'conditions and decisions made elsewhere, in the television networks, the educational system, in firms, or the labour market, or in the transportation system, with general disregard of their private, biographical consequences' (Beck, 1992: 133). He has few resources and circuits of communication that he can use to understand and negotiate the economic, financial and personal risks that face him.

And yet Glyn does have one 'local' zone of comfort and control, one extreme locus of 'individualization'. In an era which commoditizes health and sells the 'fit body', he is a triathlete. This means long hours of cycling alone. This is 'something for myself', away from his family and his work concerns. Here, unlike elsewhere in his life, he does take some risks (cycling too fast downhill, etc.). But he wears a helmet, and feels some sense of pleasure, being in control. He also has a few mates who cycle as well, and whom he meets at Penarth gym. For Glyn (but not, of course, for his wife left at home), his body is about the only major resource left to mobilize positively: 'I like to feel good. I like to keep fit, and it is an outlet different from work, different from the family, something I want to do for myself. It helps me to clear my head when it is full of crap all day. I just feel a lot better after I have done it.' In his body-focused attempt, against all these domestic and workplace 'others', to control his time and his space, Glyn's response is very similar to that of our last Cardiff/Penarth interviewee, Brian.

Brian

As a former British Olympic swimmer, Brian, 53, is an even more talented athlete than Glyn. He also worked in a very different 'traditional economy' job, as a physical education teacher in a 'welfare state' children's home. But, as has happened with a number of highly publicized former boys' home professionals in the UK, Brian seems to have become the victim of a strong fear in British society about paedophilia. He was the subject of a single accusation from a former in-care youth, who allegedly remembered an 'incident' that had occurred two decades before. The police 'trawled' other members of the boys' home from 20 years before and conducted an invasion of his home (all his videotapes were confiscated). This resulted in pressure on his family and friends and continuing suspension from his job. Brian did not go to gaol, unlike a number of other media-profiled people in his situation, because the court in this case dismissed accusations against him. Yet, his employer has refused to reinstate him and Brian fights on through the National Union of Teachers.

He describes his own current life as almost completely determined – personally, domestically, economically and socially – by what is supposed to have happened 25 years ago (as well as four years previously, when the police arrived at his door to arrest him):

> One fine morning in November 1998 I was arrested, without having done anything wrong. It sounds like the terrible opening of a Kafka novel, but the Kafkaesque surrealism has resonated through my life ever since. Basically, I have been acquitted of allegations and malicious lies in a court. I fear that my employer has been in a state of moral panic about the scale of allegations in their children's homes up and down the country, and the social workers and teachers who worked with these deprived children have become contemporary demons, and have themselves become the victims of a witch-hunt.

We have ended this chapter with Brian's story, because on the one hand it reminds us that 'traditional industries' (even in Beck's formulation) extend well beyond the coal mines and shipping of Penarth, Brian's boyhood home. It includes also, the 'care' homes of a 'welfare state' society which Ulrich Beck sees as passing. On the other hand, Brian's story (whatever the rights and wrongs of his particular case) illustrates one time/risk relationship that is profoundly determined by an area of risk to which Beck hardly refers, but which our interviewees in Cardiff, Coventry and Oxford mentioned more regularly than anything else: fear of crime, especially in relation to young people. The desire to create a more 'risk free' environment for children was a continuous theme of our Cardiff interviews, as elsewhere, and it was an underpinning factor in the 'demonization' that Brian encountered.

For Brian, the results of those past accusations have resulted in him turning back to his own body – as a former international athlete – and to the social life that his training has helped to engender:

> The gym is my therapy, it has been my antidote. It's always been an integral part of my life to go training because I competed at quite a high level. And I have found that it's been my coping mechanism in dealing with the resonance of this Kafkaesque situation that I find myself in – that I haven't done anything wrong but my employer doesn't believe me or doesn't wish to believe me. And I have had difficulty in coping with that, plus the indignity that my family have suffered. But certainly a physical regime like that in the gym has helped me. And the social aspect there is very important, the interaction – that's where you get your identity from, your peers as you interact with them, and that keeps you sane. That's been crucial. Going to the gym has increased in importance for me, without a doubt. It's been my lifeline.

But then there is the rest of Brian's 'everyday' to manage. Although unable to control the biggest risk of his life, Brian does try to control the minutiae of hours in his day:

> Every day I have an agenda. I get up fairly early, and go swimming one day and to the gym the following day, alternating through the week. Then I follow an agenda of things. I go to the Penarth museum: I'm very interested in the arts, and so that keeps me focused and stimulated. I also have friends who are musicians in the Welsh National Opera, and I am always going around to rehearsals to see these and be involved with them. I've now also become very good at house-work and gardening, which I never was before. I never have a problem filling my day, and even if the weather is very grey, and wet and dismal I have a full agenda of things to do. I have an aged mother who needs care, and friends that I see. I read a lot. So I do have a full day which keeps me, and not only my physical wellbeing but also my cognitive wellbeing as well, I think, I hope anyway. I have a check-off list of things to do. I have a diary and I plan what I'm doing for the week, and as far as I possibly can, I try to keep to those lists.

Brian has undergone his own 'disembedding' (from work, which in turn has threatened his domestic life) and 'disenchantment' (with the 'goods' of the welfare state). In particular, he certainly feels completely dominated by 'conditions and decisions made elsewhere, in the … educational system … with general disregard of their private, biographical consequences' (Beck, 1992: 133). As a result of his experience, he is even more concerned about a 'breakdown of the social fabric' among young people, than our other inter-viewees. But slowly, painstakingly and with considerable determination he has endeavoured to replace old solidarities with new ones (he is extremely visible as part of the social 'glue' at the gym, and he still competes nationally as a swimmer), and with new, routinely crucial, temporalities.

Concluding comments

We have used four analytical 'grids' in discussing in this chapter our five Cardiff case studies. First, we have drawn on the notion of 'risk biography' which we developed throughout the book. Here we argue that Beck's 'risk society' thesis was, despite its emphasis on 'individualization', not individual-everyday enough in its investigation. The risk society thesis – especially in its rhetorical posture concerning the 'cataclysmic democracy' of risk – is not sufficiently situated, not sufficiently concerned with localized 'tales from the field'. By encouraging people to speak, in long interviews, about a wide range of risk anxieties, we could see the ways in which not only different kinds of risk perception, but also different temporal-biographical stages (and memo-ries) of risk negotiation, inter-penetrate as people 'go on' with their lives.

Our first case study, Shani, is a good example of this. Here we see the way in which a focus on risk biographies can bring together personalized and cul-tural histories of time and (localized) place. We can observe an interviewee blend long-term traditions and new agencies, mix chosen and imposed hybridities, mobilize perceptions of 'then' (Shani's corner shop) and 'now' (the need for 'qualifications'). Old and new embodiments negotiate with each other, as both Shani and Karen rethink the local and national 'place' in terms of their embryonic or very young children. Risk biographies, in other words, can be a valuable methodological device for examining the 'fragmentation' profiled by post-structuralist thinking, yet in the continuing 'modernity' of most people's perceived lives.

Second, some consideration of Justin's very different risk biography, which marks out a stark contrast (compared with Shani's continuity) between his parents and his own mobility of 'place', profiles a different contrast/continuity. This particular 'grid' takes seriously Beck's account of the 'overlap' of 'class' and 'risk' modernity, within the 'unchanged logic of profit-oriented rationalization' (Beck, 1992: 149). In the British research we deliberately chose to contrast, where possible, 'traditional' and 'high tech' (or otherwise 'new economy' professionals like Jean), in order to get some sense of the everyday-situated context of Beck's 'not yet/no longer' 'system of pluralized, flexible, decentralized underemployment'. By taking three 'post-industrial cities', we could begin to examine differences (the 'local' in the 'glocal': for instance, Jean and Glyn's very different perceptions of the future of the Welsh economy; Shani and Karen's differently inflected relationship of the risks of their different local Cardiff suburb). But we could also give some empirical, 'everyday' credibility to Beck's more generalized notion of a 'risk-distributing' modernity. A significant finding of 'similarity' across all three cities has been the reflexive account among 'high-tech' workers of (precisely) Beck's two 'not yet/no longer' overlapping worlds. The confidence with which the high-tech workers greet the 'short contract', decentralized society of economic and financial risk is matched by their pessimism about the 'other' Britain that is left behind (but in some ways also threatens them) in the new 'knowledge economy'.

Third, as media and cultural theorists, we were interested in what we called the circuits of communication which people draw on in negotiating the 'individualization' of a risk society. What was most clear is that everybody does rely on other 'voices' in engaging with risk. But it is seldom the mass media which is relied upon mainly. Among 'traditional' interviewees, like Shani and Karen, the mass media are often seen as the problem: helping to generate the '20 to 30-something', 'I want' society. Both these traditional 'small shop-keepers', in their different ways, situate and contextualize the media via more trusted voices. For Shani these voices still come powerfully from her ethnic and family community (and she regrets the corner-shop talk of which proliferating supermarkets have deprived her); but she is listening also to the ('qualifications') talk of her adopted 'audit' society. Karen returns to the voices of her husband's family's culture ('Hinduism and Karma. If you don't love this woman, well you won't get a better one next time'); and on a daily basis depends on the talk of customers in her organic food shop. In her case, competing supermarkets help forge a tighter, if informal, grouping of voices in the shop; and she turns to these rather than the 'information overload' from new media and experts.

Jean, Justin and Cameron count themselves *as* experts, and have the confidence to pick and choose between other expert sources, to discriminate and be selective about the media and communication forms that they consult according to specific issues. As 'warrior class' (or at least, in distinguishing themselves from Britain's 'victim class'), they are *positively* ambivalent about science and humanity's longue duree. Rick, in contrast, positions the risks of train travel and GM food alike – together with his major risk concern of unemployment – in relation to the now ghostly voices of Beck's 'class society'. Glyn, working in the traditional and threatened industry of car accessories – and as middle-management, not unionized, even in Rick's residual way – seems the most threatened of all. He has so few voices he finds supportive: a GP in the case of his wife's illness, a mate who cut an article on Prozac and depression out of a newspaper. Beyond that, he resorts to his own silent zone, cycling long distances, taking controlled risks, working out and talking with a few gymnasium mates. In Beck's world of individualized biographies, his seems the most solipsistic.

But Glyn was not alone. Nor was this solipsism confined to his age and gender. Brian also draws deeply on the competence routines and returns of his body, and finds new social solidarities at the gym as he does so. He has educational resources, also, that Glyn and others do not, which lead him to musicians in rehearsal, theatre performers and museums to orchestrate his new temporalities of identity and control. And he reads specialist magazines and broadsheet newspapers as they probe the threats and injustices of police 'trawling' methods to identify and prosecute paedophiles, so that his own case is lit by others, and there is a sense of 'expert' light at the end of his particular, 'Kafkaesque' tunnel. Risk narratives like Glyn's and Brian's are evidence that between the society of 'no longer' powerfully unionized voices and welfare state 'goods', and the 'not yet' world of confident risk surfers and high-tech controllers, there are many ways in which people both lose and find their way.

Our fourth 'grid' relates to Beck's re-thinking of modernity, and his emphasis on the failure of 'calculability' in risk modernity. As we have seen, however, calculability is still central to everyday accounts and experiences of risk (never more evidently than in the case of Brian). It is the *positioning* of calculability which varies. For Brian, calculability relates to his careful co-ordination of bodily and daily time routines to give him a solidarity space to continue his fight. But for Jean, calculability is the mark of her long-term membership of the 'warrior class'. Beck is certainly right, however, about the reflexivity of the citizens of risk society. There is a remarkable similarity in the negative moral order described by both 'traditional' and 'new economy' interviewees: of teenage risk, alienation and loss of identity, catastrophic break-down (especially among older people used to 'a job for life'), drugs, crime, over-crowding, the greater pace of life, continuous job change, geographical mobility, and so on.

When a similar concatenation of 'bads' were revealed by social theory in the late-nineteenth century, at a time of a rampant social Darwinism, many intellectuals devised an atavistic evolutionist theory (of 'degeneration') to account for the future of this 'other' society. At the other end of the historical trajectory of 'industrial modernity', Beck and many others are unable to trust in any 'scientific' theory at all. Indeed, 'cognition' now lies at the heart of his perceived problems of immiseration. Our British research has revealed that many 'high-tech' interviewees share this notion of the association with cognitive immiseration and risk distribution. But here, too, it is a case of 'not yet/no longer'. As we have seen, those who believe they do have the cognitive skills and competences to *use and control risk* (or, as in Brian's case, to counter it) cannot easily reject 'science' altogether. Moreover, the 'no longer' continues to exist for both 'traditional' and 'high-tech' workers as a potential future of personal, social and criminal disruption.

Questions about the genetically modified food issue threw up this ambivalence clearly, especially among the 'new economy' interviewees. Jean in fact still looked back to Darwin in her sense of a progressing future; Justin and Cameron were both unable to relinquish entirely their belief in science resolving global food and pesticide problems; and Brian spoke both of GM's scientific promise to defeat world hunger and its 'health uncertainty factor'. What the case studies did support was Beck's view that it is the better educated who actively inform themselves more about environmental risk in risk modernity; and Jean seems as aware of the importance of a new sub-politics in creating a 'warrior (rather than victim) class' as Beck. However, it was also clear that – quite apart from the shifting affiliations of new, reflexive sub-political groups – knowledge defines the depth and dimensions of hazards perhaps even more powerfully in the economic than the environmental sphere. Certainly those who felt in 'control' in the risk society defined that control much more clearly in terms of economic issues rather than environmental issues (where they were, as we said, much more ambivalent).

Final Thoughts

In this book we have sought to explore the notions of 'risk society' and 'risk modernity' as they are manifested and experienced in everyday lives. Throughout, we have attempted to use our interview data, mainly in the form of 'risk biographies', to examine how lay people understand the concept of risk, how they see it as affecting their lives and those of their compatriots.

The book has been written largely in the form of a dialogue with the ideas of Ulrich Beck. We have found his writings in many ways important and insightful in bringing light to bear upon how late modern societies think about and deal with risk. It was evident from both our Australian and British interviewees' accounts that many had a heightened awareness of risk. This awareness related to a wide category of risks: principally, for our interviewees, financial, health or physical, criminal, intimate and work-related. In many respects, therefore, the people we interviewed did conform to Beck's notion of the egocentric, rationalist risk-avoider, choosing to seek out information on risk and weighing up their options. So too, his notion of individualization explains much about the disembedding aspects of everyday life, the loss of traditional ties and knowledges and the sense that 'community' is being undermined, all of which were expressed by our interviewees in both Britain and Australia.

However, we have also pointed to difficulties we have identified in Beck's work, including his overweening focus on the cognitive and individualistic aspects of risk consciousness and his generalizing tendencies. Our interviewees demonstrated an individualizing approach to risk but also a politicized social consciousness of the structural underpinnings of risks that required government intervention. Further, unlike the universal risk actor in Beck's accounts, the interviewees' reflexive responses to risk were strongly shaped via such factors as gender, age, occupation, nationality and sexual identity.

Here the works of Lash and Douglas have proved enlightening, in emphasizing the importance of aesthetic, affective and cultural aspects of risk ideas. As we noted in the Introduction, for Lash, aesthetic reflexivity is embodied in such aspects of self-interpretation as taste and style, consumption, leisure and popular culture. It involves the sophisticated processing of signs and symbols rather than simply the accumulation and assessment of 'information'.

There is an emphasis on the notion of risk knowledges as at least partly produced through consumption and commodity culture, and as inextricably interrelated with such features of selfhood as identity and membership of communities and subcultural groups.

Struggling with assessments of risk, including weighing up those espoused by experts, is part of the construction of identities – and these include, for any one individual, identities based on affect as well as cognition. Beck's notion of risk in everyday life needs to be expanded to embrace all these shifting states and performativities. Identity is constantly built and re-built through social contact and the appropriation and consumption of cultural artefacts such as technology, the media, mass-produced commodities and expert knowledges. It is also constructed through the cultural processes of which Douglas writes, including the maintenance of symbolic boundaries which outline what and who are considered to be 'dangerous' and 'Other', and thus potentially risky. We identified various ways in which the Self/Other binary opposition served to give meaning to our interviewees' understandings of risk and risk-taking.

The contradiction, ambivalence and complexity in response to risk described by Lash were apparent in our interviewees' accounts of their understandings and experiences of risk. While most people asserted that they sought to control many risks, the majority also argued for the impor- tance of deliberately taking some risks. This is an aspect of risk reflexivity that has been little acknowledged by Beck and most other risk theorists.

The discourses employed by people when describing their risk-taking, spoke of intensity of emotion and embodied sensation, of movement, flows and waves that break down or cross cultural boundaries. These tropes sug- gest that the pleasures invoked by risk-taking for some are also implicated with transgression of the 'civilized' body image. Against the ideal of the highly controlled 'civilized' body/self is the discourse which valorizes escape from the bonds of control and regulation, the body that is more permeable and open to the world. This discourse rejects the ideal of the disembodied rational actor for an ideal of the self that emphasizes heightened sensual embodiment – the visceral and emotional flights produced by encounters with danger. Yet, as we have argued, risk-taking is not only about loss of control over the body/self. For some people, notions of control remain central to risk-taking and constitute an important part of its pleasures. Indeed, if successfully undertaken without disaster striking, voluntary risk-taking can lead to a greater sense of control, resulting in a feeling of accomplishment and agency. Risk-taking, therefore, is far more complex than is suggested in most writings on risk. It may be based just as much on knowledge – of the self, of one's own bodily capacities and desires – as on ignorance.

Our study, in taking a comparative perspective, was able to demonstrate how certain aspects of risk consciousness appeared to be shared across subcultural groups but also how there were important differences between countries and between geographical regions in the same city or region. Our research has only been able to begin to address the ways in which acculturation into particular spaces and places contribute to risk understandings. More research needs to be undertaken to identify the nature of the shifting and multiple 'risk cultures' that make up 'risk modernity'.

References

Adams, J. (1995) *Risk*, London: UCL Press.

Alexander, J. (1996) 'Critical reflections on "reflexive modernization"', *Theory, Culture & Society*, 13: 133–8.

Allan, S., Adam, B. and Carter, C. (eds) (2000) *Media, Risk and the Environment*, London: UCL.

Beck, U. (1992) *Risk Society: Towards a New Modernity*, London: Sage.

Beck, U. (1994) 'The reinvention of politics: towards a theory of reflexive modernization', in U. Beck, A. Giddens and S. Lash, *Reflexive Modernization: Politics, Tradition and Aesthetics in the Modern Social Order*, Cambridge: Polity Press, pp. 1–55.

Beck, U. (1995) *Ecological Politics in the Age of Risk*, Cambridge: Polity Press.

Beck, U. (2000a) 'Risk society revisited: theory, politics and research programmes', in B. Adam, U. Beck and J. Van Loon (eds), *The Risk Society and Beyond*, London: Sage, pp. 211–29.

Beck, U. (2000b) 'Preface', in S. Allan, B. Adam, and C. Carter (eds), *Media, Risk and the Environment*, London: UCL, pp. xii–xiv.

Beck, U. and Beck-Gernsheim, E. (1995) *The Normal Chaos of Love*, Cambridge: Polity Press.

Boholm, A. and Lofstedt, R. (1999) 'Issues of risk, trust and knowledge: the Hallandsas Tunnell case', *Ambio*, 28(6): 556–61.

Boyne, R. (1998) 'The politics of risk society', *History of the Human Sciences*, 11(3): 15–30.

Brooks, R. and Holbrook, B. (1998) '"Mad cows and Englishmen". Gender implications of news reporting on the British beef crisis', in C. Carter, G. Branston and S. Allan (eds), *News, Gender and Power*. London: Routledge, pp. 174–85.

Butz, D. and Leslie, D. (2000) 'Risky subjects: changing geographies of employment in the automobile industry', paper presented at the Association of American Geographers, Pittsburg, USA.

Canaan, J. (1996) '"One thing leads to another": drinking, fighting and working-class masculinities', in M. Mac an Ghaill (ed.), *Understanding Masculinities*, Buckingham: Open University Press, pp. 114–25.

Caplan, P. (2000) '"Eating British beef with confidence": a consideration of consumers' responses to BSE in Britain', in P. Caplan (ed.), *Risk Revisited*, London: Pluto Press, pp. 184–203.

Cohen, M. (2000) 'Environmental sociology, social theory and risk: an introductory discussion', in M. Cohen (ed.), *Risk in the Modern Age: Social Theory, Science and Environmental Decision-Making*, Basingstoke: Macmillan, pp. 3–31.

Collison, M. (1996) 'In search of the high life: drugs, crime, masculinities and consumption', *British Journal of Criminology*, 36(3): 428–44.

Douglas, M. (1966) *Purity and Danger: An Analysis of Concepts of Pollution and Taboo*, London: Routledge & Kegan Paul.

Douglas, M. (1992) *Risk and Blame: Essays in Cultural Theory*, London: Routledge.

Eder, K. (2000) 'Taming risks through dialogues: the rationality and functionality of discursive institutions in risk society', in M. Cohen (ed.), *Risk in the Modern Age: Social Theory, Science and Environmental Decision-Making*, Basingstoke: Macmillan, pp. 225–48.

Ekinsmyth, C. (2000) 'Ambivalence and paradox: freelancing in a risk society', paper presented at the Association of American Geographers, Pittsburg, USA.

Finucane, M., Slovic, P., Mertz, C., Flynn, J. and Satterfield, T. (2000) 'Gender, race and perceived risk: the "white male" effect', *Health, Risk & Society*, 2(2): 159–72.

Foucault, M. (1988) 'Technologies of the self', in L. Martin, H. Gutman and P. Hutton (eds), *Technologies of the Self: A Seminar with Michel Foucault*, London: Tavistock, pp. 16–49.

Giddens, A. (1992) *The Transformation of Intimacy: Sexuality, Love and Eroticism in Modern Societies*, Cambridge: Polity Press.

Hage, G. (1997) 'At home in the entrails of the West', in H. Grace, G. Hage, L. Johnson, J. Langsworthy and M. Symonds (eds), *Home World: Space, Community and Marginality in Sydney's West*, Sydney: Pluto Press.

Hansson, S. (1989) 'Dimensions of risk', *Risk Analysis*, 9(1): 107–12.

Hargreaves, J. (1997) 'Women's boxing and related activities: introducing images and meanings', *Body & Society*, 3(4): 33–50.

Hassin, J. (1994) 'Living a responsible life: the impact of AIDS on the social identity of intravenous drug users', *Social Science of Medicine*, 39(3): 391–400.

Lash, S. (1993) 'Reflexive modernization: the aesthetic dimension', *Theory, Culture & Society*, 10: 1–23.

Lash, S. (2000) 'Risk culture', in B. Adam, U. Beck and J. Van Loon (eds), *The Risk Society and Beyond*, London: Sage, pp. 47–62.

Lash, S. and Wynne, B. (1992) 'Introduction', in U. Beck, *Risk Society: Towards a New Modernity*, London: Sage, pp. 1–8.

Lidskog, R. (2000) 'Scientific evidence or lay people's experiences? On risk and trust with regard to modern environmental threats', in M. Cohen (ed.), *Risk in the Modern Age: Social Theory, Science and Environmental Decision-Making*, Basingstoke: Macmillan, pp. 196–224.

Lopes, L. (1991) 'The rhetoric of irrationality', *Theory & Psychology*, 1: 65–82.

Lovering, J. (1999) 'Theory led by policy: the inadequacies of the "New Regionalism" illustrated from the case of Wales', *International Journal of Urban and Regional Research*, 23(2): 379–95.

Lupton, D. (1998) *The Emotional Self: A Sociocultural Exploration*, London: Sage.

Lupton, D. (1999) *Risk*, London: Routledge.

Lyng, S. (1978) 'Edgework: a social psychological analysis of voluntary risk taking', *American Journal of Sociology*, 95(4): 851–86.

Maticka-Tyndale, E. (1992) 'Social construction of HIV transmission and prevention among heterosexual young adults', *Social Problems*, 39(3): 238–52.

Miller, D. (1999) 'Risk, science and policy: definitional struggles, information management, the media and BSE', *Social Science & Medicine*, 49: 1239–55.

Murcott, A. (1999) '"Not science but PR": GM food and the makings of a considered sociology', *Sociological Research Online*, 4(3).

Skidmore, D. and Hayter, E. (2000) 'Risk and sex: ego-centricity and sexual behaviour in young adults', *Health, Risk & Society*, 2(1): 23–32.

Slovic, P. (1987) 'Perception of risk', *Science*, 236: 280–5.

Stranger, M. (1999) 'The aesthetics of risk: a study of surfing', *International Review for the Sociology of Sport*, 34(3): 265–76.

Tulloch, J. (1992) 'Discoursing AIDS and sexuality', *Social Semiotics*, 2(2): 113–51.

Wynne, B. (1989) 'Frameworks of rationality in risk management: towards the testing of naive sociology', in J. Brown (ed.), *Environmental Threats: Perception, Analysis and Management*, London: Belhaven Press, pp. 33–47.

Wynne, B. (1996) 'May the sheep safely graze? A reflexive view of the expert-lay knowledge divide', in S. Lash, B. Szerszinski and B. Wynne (eds), *Risk, Environment and Modernity: Towards a New Ecology*, London: Sage, pp. 44–83.

Index

Aboriginal people 26, 27
adrenalin 34–5
aesthetic reflexivity 6
age
  border crossings 41–2, 52–4, 55, 91–2
  control 31
  health 23
  loneliness 52–4, 55
  responsibilities 19–20, 24–5
Alexander, J. 7
asset-stripping 68
asylum seeking 27, 92
avoidance
  control 10, 29
  responsibilities 20–1, 24–5
  sociocultural meanings 8

Beck, Ulrich 1–7
Beck-Gernsheim, E. 1
bias, sociocultural meanings 8
biographical data 14
biography 61–80
blame
  government 27, 125
  individualization 4, 29, 118–19
  individuals 93, 98, 102–3
  media 68, 129
  reflexive modernization 4, 27
  Thatcherism 68, 75, 123–4, 125
border crossings 41–60
  see also age; immigration; sexual preference
  class structure 43
  community 46, 48, 54
  ethnicity 95–9
  plural rationalities 103–5
boundary crossings, globalization 64–5, 67–8
BSE see mad cow disease
Butz, D. 64–5, 67–8

calculability
  see also incalculability

calculability, cont.
  capitalism 65
  control 35
  financial risk 71
  modernity 130
capitalism 5, 62, 65, 75–6, 86–91
Caplan, P. 9
catalysts for change 43–4
children see families
citizenship 68
class structure 29–31, 43, 79, 98
comfort zones 33
community
  border crossings 46, 48, 54
  individualization 109–10
  risk modern cities 109–10
  supermarkets 112, 113, 129
  wartime 83–4
competition 119–20
confidence 31
conservatism 20
consumerism 47–8, 61, 63, 91, 110–11
control
  age 31
  avoidance 10, 29
  confidence 31
  crime 70–1
  cultural capital 29–32
  emotion 37
  financial risk 71–2
  gender 31
  job security 66–7, 124
  minimizing risks 30
corporatist economies 81–2
cost-cutting 76, 86, 92
crime
  control 70–1
  discrimination 22, 56–7
  fear 21, 28, 85
cultivated risk-taking 36
cultural capital 29–32

cultural dispositions 6–7, 8
cultural risk 97
cultural subgroups 6

decentralization 62
decision-making 7
  confidence 31
  families 70
  trust 9
democracies, freedom 46, 48
dialogical incrementalism 82–3
diaspora 41, 43–4
diet 30
discrimination 22–3, 56–7
disenchantment 107, 110–13, 117, 128
divisiveness 26–7, 44
Douglas, Mary 6–7, 38, 42, 132–3

Eder, Klaus 81–3
edgework 33–4, 36
Ekinsmyth, C. 63–4
embedded knowledge 9, 45
embedded risk 89, 107, 110, 128
emotion 18–19, 23–4, 34–5, 37
employment
  changing 20–1, 22
  class structure 30
  corporate loyalty 93–5
  decentralization 62
  job security 28, 30–2, 66–8, 123–5
  market changes 27–9, 62–3, 71–2,
    86, 108, 116, 122
  occupational risk 23, 86–7, 101, 124
  retraining 22
  underemployment 62, 77, 110–11
  unemployment 2, 4, 26, 27
  unions 123–4
environmental risk 2, 13
  Australian perspective 26, 39
  British perspective 39
  globalization 69, 75, 76
  invisibility 82, 113
ethnicity 95–9
experts 118
  health 98
  lay risk knowledges 3, 9
  learning 53–4
  media 98
extreme sports 10–11, 20, 34–6, 45, 72, 81

families
  see also community
  border crossings 49–50
  breakdown 2, 24, 96, 109–10, 122
  decision-making 70

families, cont.
  immigration 108–9
  individualization 4
  marriage 23–4
  media 93
  mobility 63, 119
  responsibilities 20–1, 24–5, 32
  settling down 20, 38
fatalism 32
financial risk 24, 26, 89–90
  constraints 72, 81
  consumerism 47–8
  cost-cutting 76, 86, 92
  investment 95
  market changes 86
  pay-off 71
Finucane, M. 8
food contamination 2, 10
freedom, democracies 46, 48
fulfilment 34

gender 20
  control 31
  relationships 53–4
  shared risk 21
  voluntary risk-taking 22, 33–4
genetically modified (GM) foods 13–14,
  69–70, 73–5, 76
globalization
  Australian perspective 39
  boundary crossing 64–5, 67–9
  environmental risk 69, 75, 76
  individualization 4
  risk society 2
'glocal' issues 2, 12
GM see genetically modified

Hanson, Pauline 26
health
  abroad 99
  age 23
  computers 86
  diet 30
  experts 98
  GM foods 13–14, 69–70, 73–5, 76
  HIV/AIDS 8–9, 22–3, 44–5,
    51–2, 55, 90
  insurance 47, 86
  lifestyle 30, 56
  safe sex 45, 51–2
  smoking 72–3
heuristics 8
HIV/AIDS 8–9, 22–3, 44–5,
  51–2, 55, 90
hybridity 63

immigration
  border crossings 41–2, 43–4, 46, 49–50
  families 108–9
  social impact 41
incalculability 69, 74
individualization 4, 38, 61–80
  blame 118–19
  community 109–10
  embedded risk 107, 110, 128
  media 61–2
  resistance 63
information overload 114, 115
investments see financial risk
invisibility 69–70, 75, 77, 82, 113

job security 28, 66–8, 123–5

knowledge 1
  embedded 9
  experts 3, 9
  learning 53–4
  media 88

Lash, S. 6, 132–3
lay people 1, 3, 7–11
learning 53–4
Leslie, D. 64–5, 67–8
Lidskog, R. 81, 82–3, 84
lifestyle 30, 56
loneliness 52–4, 55
Lovering, J. 108
Lyng, S. 33–4

mad cow disease (BSE) 9–10, 39, 73–4, 81
manipulation, media 47, 55
marginalized groups 7, 8
marriage 23–4
mass media see media
materialism 91, 110–11, 113
media
  blame 68, 129
  discrimination 123, 130
  experts 98
  families 93
  imagistic power 5
  individualization 61–2
  information overload 114, 115
  information sources 59
  manipulation 47, 55
  sensationalism 74–5, 82
  trust 87–8, 100, 115
  witchhunts 126–7
Miller, D. 64
minimizing risks 30
mobility 14, 119

modernity 61–80
  calculability 130
  individualization 4
  risk modern cities 106–31
  risk society 2–4
monitoring risks 117, 120
moral risks 6–7
multicultural societies 41, 42–3

negativity 17–18, 45
New Labour 125
non-control see control

occupational risk 23, 86–7, 101, 124
over-population 114–15

pay-off 71
peers, trust 100
personal biography 38
pesticides, food contamination 2
physical endangerment 17–18, 31, 56,
  99–102
plural rationalities 81–105
pollution see environmental risk
population growth 114–15
positivity 18, 45
post-modernism 55, 59
power 63–4, 69
powerful allusion 64
private reflexivity 7–11

racial issues
  Aboriginal people 26, 27
  asylum seeking 27, 92
  diaspora 41, 43–4
rationalities, plural 81–105
re-nationalization 123
rebellion 52–3
reflexive biography 4, 44, 48, 50, 54
reflexive modernization 2, 3, 4
rejection 23–4
relationships 23–4, 53–4
responsibilities
  age 19–20, 24–5
  blame 29
  control 29
  families 20–1, 24–5, 32
ridicule 24
risk assessment 1
risk cultures 6
risk management 1
risk modern cities 106–31
risk society 2–7
Risk Society: Towards a New Modernity
  (Beck) 1, 61

risk-taking
  see also avoidance; voluntary risk-taking
  class structure 29–32
  control 10–11, 32–6
  gender 22
  as human condition 72, 81
  as movement 33
  pleasure 32–6, 37, 133
  sociocultural meanings 8

self-actualization 19, 34, 37–8
settling down 20, 38
sexual activity 8–9, 22–3, 51, 55, 90
sexual preference 22–3, 41–2, 44–5, 50–7
shared risk 20–1
short-term risk 22
sociocultural meanings 8, 9
spatial metaphors 33, 38
spatial mobility 14, 119
Stranger, M. 35
synoptic planning 82–3

taking control *see* control
Thatcherism 68, 75, 123–4, 125

trust
  decision-making 9
  government 69–70, 87–8, 100
  media 87–8, 100, 114–15
  peers 100
  scientific data 117

uncertainty 3, 17, 106
underemployment 62, 77, 110–11
unemployment 2, 4, 26, 27

victim culture 121–2
voluntary risk-taking
  control 11
  emotion 34–5, 37
  gender 22
  pleasure 32–6, 37, 104

warrior class 116–18, 130
work *see* employment
world risk society 2, 74
worldviews 8, 19
Wynne, Brian 7, 9